The Making of the Twentieth Century

This series of specially commissioned titles focuses attention on significant and often controversial events and themes of world history in the present century. The authors, many of them already outstanding in their field, have tried to close the gap between the intelligent layman, whose interest is aroused by recent history, and the specialist student at university. Each book will therefore provide sufficient narrative and explanation for the newcomer while offering the specialist student detailed source-references and bibliographies, together with interpretation and reassessment in the light of recent scholarship.

In the choice of subjects there will be a balance between breadth in some spheres and detail in others; between the essentially political and matters scientific, economic or social. The series cannot be a comprehensive account of everything that has happened in the twentieth century, but it will provide a guide to recent research and explain something of the times of extraordinary change and complexity in which we live.

The Making of the Twentieth Century

Series Editor: CHRISTOPHER THORNE

Other titles in the Series include

Already published

Coming shortly

In preparation

The Age of Containment

The Cold War 1945–1965

David Rees

There are two things a prince should fear: internal subversion
from his subjects; and external aggression by foreign powers.
Against the latter, his defence lies in being well armed and having
good allies; and if he is well armed he will always have good allies.
In addition, domestic affairs will always remain under control
provided that relations with external powers are under control
and so long as they have not already been disturbed by conspiracy. Even if there is disturbance abroad, if the prince has
ordered his government . . . and if he does not capitulate he will
always repulse every onslaught. . . .

The Prince

Macmillan

London · Melbourne · Toronto

St Martin's Press

New York

1 9 6 8

© David Rees 1967

First published 1967
Reprinted 1968

Published by
MACMILLAN AND CO LTD
Little Essex Street London WC2
and also at Bombay Calcutta and Madras
Macmillan South Africa (Publishers) Pty Ltd Johannesburg
The Macmillan Company of Australia Pty Ltd Melbourne
The Macmillan Company of Canada Ltd Toronto
St Martin's Press Inc New York

Library of Congress catalog card no. 67–10650

Printed in Great Britain by
ROBERT MACLEHOSE AND CO LTD
The University Press, Glasgow

TO

Anthony Hartley

Contents

Plates and Maps

The cover picture shows President Kennedy and Chairman Khrushchev talking together at their Vienna meeting, June 1961.

PLATES

between pages 84 and 85

The author and publishers wish to thank the following for
permission to reproduce the plates: cover picture, 1*a*, *b*, United
States Information Service; 2*a*, United States State Department; 2*b*, United States Army; 3*a*, United States Marine
Corps; 3*b*, United States Defence Department; 4, 5, F.C.I.
News Agency; 6*a*, *b*, 7*a*, United States Air Force; 8, Institute
of Strategic Studies.

MAPS

The author and publishers wish to thank the following for
permission to reproduce the maps:

Map 1: H.M.S.O., based on *The Meaning of Berlin* (1962).

Map 2: based on maps from *The White House Years*: vol. i,
Mandate for Change, and vol. ii, *Waging Peace*, by Dwight D.
Eisenhower (London, Heinemann, 1963), by permission
of Messrs. Doubleday & Co. Inc., New York; *The Red
Army of China*, by Edgar O'Ballance (London, Faber &
Faber, 1962); and *Time*, 7 January 1966.

Map 3: Messrs. Faber & Faber, based on maps from *The
Red Army of China*, by Edgar O'Ballance (1962).

Map 4: based on a map from *Time*, 7 January 1966.

Map 5: based on a map from *Time*, 2 November 1962.

ACKNOWLEDGEMENT

The author and publishers wish to thank Messrs. William
Heinemann Ltd., and Messrs. Doubleday & Co. Inc., New
York, for permission to use extracts from *The White House
Years*, vol. i, *Mandate for Change*, by Dwight D. Eisenhower
(1963).

Abbreviations

AEC	(United States) Atomic Energy Commission
ANF	Atlantic Nuclear Force
CCF	Chinese Communist Forces
CCP	Chinese Communist Party
CENTO	Central Treaty Organisation
CIA	(United States) Central Intelligence Agency
Cominform	Communist Information Bureau
Comintern	Third Communist International
CPSU	Communist Party of the Soviet Union
EDC	European Defence Community
EEC	European Economic Community
ELAS	Greek Communist guerrilla fighters
GDR	German Democratic Republic
ICBM	Inter-continental ballistic missile
IRBM	Intermediate-range ballistic missile
KMT	Kuomintang
MIG	Russian jet fighter aircraft
MLF	Multilateral Force
MRBM	Medium-range ballistic missile
NATO	North Atlantic Treaty Organisation
NKVD	Narodny Kommisariat Vnuttrennikh Del, (Soviet) People's Commissariat of Internal Affairs, now succeeded by KGB, Komitet Gosudarstsvennoie Bezopasnosti, State Security Committee
NSC	(United States) National Security Council
OAS	Organisation of American States
RAND	Research and Development Corporation
ROK	Republic of Korea
SAC	Strategic Air Command
SACEUR	Supreme Allied Commander, Europe
SEATO	South-East Asia Treaty Organisation
SED	Socialist Unity Party (East Germany)
SPD	Social Democratic Party
SHAPE	Supreme Headquarters Allied Powers Europe
US	United States
USAF	United States Air Force
VE Day	Victory in Europe Day
VJ Day	Victory in Japan Day
WEU	Western European Union

Introduction
The Gigantic Civil War

IN spite of the nuclear stalemate between East and West, the Soviet and Chinese leaders frequently state that history is on their side. Yet nearly a hundred years before the phrase 'cold war' was born in 1947 to describe the present conflict between the Communist countries and the Western powers, Marx and Engels in the *Communist Manifesto* (1848) had flung down a challenge to the bourgeois world-system that today echoes from the remotest parts of the earth: 'The communists everywhere support every revolutionary movement against the existing social and political order. . . . The communists disdain to conceal their views and aims. They openly declare that their ends can only be attained by the overthrow of all existing social conditions. . . .'

Thus we can see that there are good grounds for thinking that the intellectual origins of the cold war may be traced back to the *Communist Manifesto*. And there can be little doubt that the conflict as we know it today stems from the events of 7 November 1917, with the successful storming of the Petrograd Winter Palace by Trotsky's Red Guards, followed by Lenin's fateful words uttered the next day to the Second All-Russian Congress of Soviets: 'We shall now proceed to construct the socialist order.' As the German Marxist leader Rosa Luxemburg wrote a year later, in December 1918: 'The struggle for socialism is the most gigantic civil war world history has ever known, and the proletarian revolution must provide the tools for civil war. . . .' In the next twenty-five years, as the Soviet régime became consolidated under Stalin's direction, there were

successive crises, such as the forcible collectivisation of
agriculture, the destruction of the richer peasants or kulaks,
and the Great Purges of the 1930s which finally destroyed
the Old Bolsheviks. When Hitler attacked the USSR in
June 1941 it seemed for a few weeks as if Stalin's Russia
would be destroyed.

But within less than two years of the German attack on
Russia it became clear, with the great Soviet victory at
Stalingrad in January 1943, that the USSR would be one
of the two great powers of the post-war world. By the time
of the last war-time Allied conference, at Potsdam in July
1945, some Western leaders saw that there were grave differences between the Anglo-American powers and the Soviet
Union; and with the emergence of President Truman's
doctrine of aid to Greece and Turkey in March 1947
came the phrase that has survived ever since to describe the
conflict between East and West.

Obviously, the prospect of indefinite tension between
East and West merits some brief assessment of the aims of
the protagonists in the conflict that has dominated international relations since 1945. Yet from the voluminous texts
of the Marxist–Leninist classics (and perhaps we should
note here that Marxism has evolved into Marxism–Leninism, as the original thought of Marx and Engels has been
interpreted by Lenin and Stalin) we can see that the cold
war represents not the newest of struggles but the oldest. It
is a contemporary form of the debate that reaches back to
the beginning of Western political thought, with the original
quest for Utopia in Plato's *Republic*. Thus the present version
of the search for Utopia by Communists, has led to a situation in which an imperfect Western society, but one with
tremendous potential for improvement, is faced with a rival
order that is perhaps the most dangerous tyranny in
history for the very reason that its highly sophisticated
techniques of repression and mendacity are justified by
ostensibly humanist ideals. One has only to read the novels

of Koestler, Silone, Malraux, or the confessionals of Whittaker Chambers or Wolfgang Leonhard to see the immense hold that this vision has had on its adherents.

It is relevant to recall here that Marx was originally concerned with the betterment of the new 'third' estate created by the industrial revolution, which he realised opened up unprecedented opportunities for raising the material standard of living. But his synthesis, combining his Hegelian philosophy of dialectical materialism, his theory of economics based on the conception of surplus value, and his analysis of the state and its role in historical development, was not only a blueprint for the betterment of the proletariat but also for the scientific *modernisation* of the world. And, if there is one scarlet thread that runs through the whole development of Marxist thought it is that the salvation of man can be brought about by science. So powerful has this intellectual synthesis of Communism been, that we can now see that Marx is the founder of the greatest mass movement since Christianity, a movement that in the mid-1960s rules a billion people in fourteen states, including Cuba and Yugoslavia. And indeed, there are many people living in many walks of life in the West today who pay more than lip service to the Communist view of world history, while not necessarily following the immediate zig-zags of the Party line.

However, it should be noted here that the theoretical basis of society in the countries of the Communist world is not that 'higher phase' of Communism governed by the principle of 'from each according to his ability, to each according to his needs'. Lenin, Stalin, and Khrushchev have followed Marx in that they all agree that the society which will invariably be established on the immediate ruins of capitalism and imperialism will be socialism, where men are still governed by the principle of 'from each according to his ability, to each according to his work'. But Marxist–Leninists call themselves Communists in order to show to the whole world that they have nothing to do with the Social Democrats, whom they have despised as part and parcel of the bourgeois world ever since Marx anathematised Louis Blanc.

Yet from the beginning of what the Soviet leaders describe as the 'world socialist system', the Utopian ends of the international Communist movement have been pitilessly subordinated to the seeking and retention of power, a process which since 1917 has led to the Protean forms of repression that we can see documented by the Communists themselves in such sources as Khrushchev's 'secret speech' of 1956. Moreover, for three reasons, the cold war is not like the conflicts of the past which ended in 1945.

In the first place, onto the often irreconcilable conflicts between states, faiths and coalitions, such as have always occurred in history — even if Russia and China were non-Communist states there would be serious differences between the maritime Western powers and the Eurasian countries — have been imposed the tensions which arise from the distinctive Communist conviction that the Party speaks for history, and that every possible means must be exploited to hasten the downfall of an imperialist system that is predictably dying from its own contradictions.

In the second place, the Soviet system under Stalin developed into a tyranny that was not like previous autocracies. Soviet Russia, and subsequently the other Communist states, became *totalitarian* societies where every aspect of human life was subordinated to the will of the Party. A close historical parallel to them lies in Hitler's Germany, which, however, possessed all the weaknesses of a National Socialist creed founded on manifestly lunatic themes of racial superiority, and which lacked the formidable propaganda advantages of the perverted humanism of Marxism–Leninism. Moreover, modern totalitarianism is something unique in history in that reality itself is transformed by it. In a modern totalitarian society, opponents are not merely eliminated, they cease to exist. The very name of Beria is erased from the history books and the encyclopaedias; Khrushchev, the ruler of the USSR for nearly ten years, becomes an 'unperson'; the mighty Stalin himself is expunged from the records. Other dictatorships have tried to control the present and the future; Communist totalitarianism has actually succeeded in remaking the past. George Orwell, in *1984*, has left an enduring testimony to the nature of contemporary totalitarianism:

> To know and not to know, to be conscious of complete truthfulness while telling carefully constructed lies, to hold simultaneously two opinions which cancelled out, knowing them to be contradictory and believing in both of them; to use logic against logic, to repudiate morality while laying claim to it, to believe that democracy was impossible and that the Party was the guardian of democracy, to forget whatever it was necessary to forget, then to draw it back into memory against the moment when it was needed, and then promptly to forget it again; above all, to apply the same process to the process itself. That was the ultimate subtlety; consciously to induce unconsciousness, and then, once again, to become unconscious of the act of hypnosis you had performed. . . . Power is not a means, it is an end. One does not establish a dictatorship in order to safeguard the revolution; one makes the revolution in order to establish the dictatorship. The object of torture is torture. The object of power is power. . . .

The inescapable lesson of twentieth-century totalitarianism is that, given control of the security apparatus, almost anything is possible.

Thirdly, the cold war is unlike the conflicts of the past because of the existence of nuclear weapons. As we all know, the nature of these weapons means that war will destroy East and West indiscriminately; yet at the same time nuclear weapons are essential in the defence of the West, for the combination of Communist totalitarianism and the threat of nuclear weapons against an unarmed West might well result in an irreversible defeat for free institutions.

Fortunately, since Stalin's death, and especially since the Cuban missile crisis — Stalin himself never embarked on such a desperate adventure as that of the ostensibly 'liberal' Khrushchev in 1962 — the Soviet leaders, if not the men of Peking, have realised that the unrestricted pursuance of their expansionist policies might well result in nuclear war. That is why they have evolved their 'coexistence' strategy, which, as we shall see in these pages, is but a strategy to achieve the desired end of world Communism by peaceful means. And increasingly, as a result of the nuclear deadlock, the Communist states are coming to deal with the West on the basis of national self-interest rather than of the fundamentalist theories of Marxism–Leninism. At the same time many of the leaders of the 'uncommitted' nations in the countries of the 'third world' have realised that Communism is the deadly enemy of the nationalism that provides so powerful a propellant to their policies, and that their own interest lies in avoiding any firm commitment to the Eastern bloc. Even inside the Communist world it has become increasingly obvious that official ideology can no longer cope with the extremely complex problems raised by modern technology, and many of the difficulties of the Party in the realms of agriculture, defence and industrial organisation are proofs of Orwell's perception that contemporary Communism is not a rational but an irrational creed. Moreover, there are indications that many Communist artists and intellectuals have fully realised that the totalitarian state, no matter what its ostensible goals of human betterment, results not in the elevation of man but his obliteration. There is nothing in the record of the last twenty years to show that a Communist victory is inevitable, as the Party's ideologues proclaim.

However, it should be noted here that the very expression 'cold war' has been consistently manipulated by Communist propaganda in the best traditions of Orwell's 'Newspeak'. We have used the term 'cold war' throughout this study as describing the interlocking series of events of the East-West conflict of the last generation. In this view the cold war includes the sum of both Soviet and Western activities. But in Communist terminology the cold war is something the imperialists do. The Moscow and Peking régimes consider that they are not the instigators, but the victims of the cold war. Thus when the Communists demand the end of the cold war, they are asking for an act of strategic surrender from the West. For what we in the West would describe as Communist subversion, conspiracy or aggression, Marxist–Leninists describe as 'the struggle for peace', 'the international class struggle' or 'the policy of peaceful coexistence'.

From such examples of Communist-inspired semantics we can see why this historicist doctrine when grafted onto the unstable nature of inter-state relations results in a greatly increased level of international tension. To counter this development Western policy in general and United States policy in particular has had over the last twenty years the objective of creating a new world balance of power, with the end of eventually reaching some sort of accommodation with the Communist powers. The basis of this Western policy has been the containment policy, inspired by George Kennan, adopted by the Truman administration in 1947, and followed in one way or another by successive US administrations ever since. And just as we have seen that the ideological debate between the adversaries in the cold war has ancient precedents, so the containment policy represents for our time a classical balance of power strategy such as great powers have always developed throughout history.

Inevitably the containment policy has achieved its greatest successes when Western policy and power have been closely integrated, rather than when rhetoric and vain hopes of 'victory' in the cold war have led Western spokesmen to misunderstand the essentially defensive nature of the containment policy, with its objective of preserving the status quo and encouraging as far as possible the survival of free institutions. Thus an Acheson has operated with greater effectiveness than a Dulles, just as the Kennedy of the 1962 Cuban missile crisis was more effective than the Kennedy of the 1961 Bay of Pigs episode. Paradoxically, it was Mr Khrushchev, who, during the Berlin crisis of 1961, saw that the Communist powers for their part violated the containment policy at their peril. In August of that year he stated: 'The experience of history teaches that when an aggressor sees that he is not being opposed he grows more brazen. Contrariwise, when he meets opposition, he calms down. It is this historic experience that must guide us in our actions.'

Nearly twenty years after the promulgation of the containment policy in 1947, George Kennan discussed his original ideas in the Vietnam hearings before the US Senate Foreign Relations Committee which took place in February 1966. Kennan remarked that of course in 1947 there was only one centre of Communist power, and that he should have emphasised at that earlier time that certain areas of the world were more important to the West than others; it was imperative to concentrate on the vital theatres of conflict. But, Kennan summed up, 'I still consider that containment is better than war, both with regard to Russia and with regard to China....' The elements of time, chance, and personality make the future course of the cold war impossible to predict with any certainty, yet surely the best hope for attaining a truce in the gigantic civil war lies in the careful application of the containment policy by the West. There can be little doubt that for the foreseeable future we shall be living in an age of containment.

1 1945-1949
A World Restored

'LET us not be deceived — today we are in the midst of a cold war.' The words were spoken by Bernard Baruch, the veteran American statesman, in Columbia, South Carolina, on 16 April 1947, a month after the promulgation of the Truman Doctrine of aid to Greece and Turkey. The phrase was taken up by Walter Lippmann in his syndicated column and immediately passed into the language as a metaphor accurately describing the situation that had arisen between the Western powers and the Soviet Union by the spring of 1947.

But as we have seen in one way or another, a cold war had been waged ever since the establishment of the Bolshevik régime in 1917. Certainly, since the great Soviet victory at Stalingrad (now Volgograd) at the beginning of 1943, we can see the conflict taking shape in its present form. In April of that year, following the discovery at Katyn, near Smolensk, of the mass graves of 5,000 Polish officers in all probability murdered by the Soviet security police (the NKVD),[1] relations were broken off between Moscow and the Polish government-in-exile in London. The climax of the Allied offensive against Germany, concerted in the first Summit held between Churchill, Roosevelt and Stalin at Tehran in November 1943 (which historians generally assume marks the high-point in Roosevelt's war-time diplomacy) and reaching its final phase with the Anglo-

[1] See J. K. Zawodny, *Deaths in the Forest* (1963), for a full treatment of the Katyn evidence.

American landings in Normandy in June 1944, tended to obscure the relentless emergence of these irreconcilable inter-allied differences.

In July 1944, as Soviet troops entered Polish territory, Moscow set up its own Polish administration, the Lublin Committee, and throughout 1944 there was growing tension behind the façade of the grand alliance of the Western allies and the Soviet Union over Italy, the future of Eastern Europe, Germany, Yugoslavia and Greece, where in December the Communist partisans of ELAS were only prevented from staging a successful take-over in Athens by British troops. Seeing the dangers of this nascent East–West rivalry, Winston Churchill had optimistically attempted in his meeting with Stalin in October 1944 to define spheres-of-influence in the Balkans, while maintaining the independence of Poland, a country which, sandwiched between Germany and Russia, was the key to the post-war power balance in central Europe. In Churchill's mind, as we can see from his history of the Second World War, was the question: could legitimate Russian interests be separated from the Communist mission to impose Soviet rule on as many countries as possible?

The answer would soon be made known, but not until after the Yalta Conference of February 1945. By this time, as the Allied armies moved into Germany, the question of Soviet participation in the Pacific war and the form of a post-war European settlement had become acute. Moscow had already recognised the Lublin Committee, now transferred to Warsaw, as the legal government of Poland in January 1945. But so great had been the upheaval caused by Germany's bid for world conquest that many Allied leaders still believed that Roosevelt's 'Grand Design', which assumed Big Three unity in peace as well as war, might be possible. And, indeed, the decisions made at Yalta affect the world to this day, though not in the way that many of the Western participants hoped. As far as Germany was concerned, the Big Three approved plans for occupation zones and for an Allied Control Commission, including the French, while the 'Declaration on Liberated Europe' reaffirmed the principles of the Atlantic Charter, promising the liberated countries and Axis satellites democratic institutions of their own choice, although no safeguards were agreed. Stalin promised that the USSR would participate in the forthcoming San Francisco Conference to draft the United Nations Charter, while all three leaders agreed on the big-power veto in the proposed UN Security Council.

But perhaps the least defensible parts of the Yalta Agreement were those relating to the Far East, made between Roosevelt and Stalin. Stalin promised to enter the Pacific war 'two or three months' after Germany's defeat; he was to be rewarded with the Kuriles and southern Sakhalin from Japan, and from China with special rights in Port Arthur and Darien, joint control of the principal Manchurian railways, and the preservation of 'the *status quo* in Outer Mongolia', a Soviet Satellite territory since the 1920s.

As for the Poles, we have it on Churchill's word that the subject was 'discussed at no fewer than seven of the eight plenary meetings' at Yalta; it was agreed that the 'Provisional Government of Poland' (the successor to the Lublin Committee) should be expanded 'on a broader democratic basis' and that free elections be held. The Russians were to be given the Curzon Line as their new Polish frontier, an arrangement that had been provisionally agreed between the three leaders at Tehran, without Polish concurrence of course, while Poland's frontier with Germany was to be moved westwards, possibly to the Oder, although no final agreement was reached on this. The world had effectively been remade in seven days at the Livadia Palace — mostly to Stalin's advantage, as events proved.

Both Roosevelt and Churchill strongly defended the

settlement on their return home, Roosevelt even telling Congress that balance-of-power policies were a thing of the past. It has often been claimed by the defenders of the settlement that Stalin was given nothing he could not have taken, but the real charge against Yalta is that Stalin was given the right to take what he did. How could the Allies later condemn Soviet interference in Poland and elsewhere, if they had sanctioned Soviet spheres-of-influence in China? Again, Roosevelt's responsibility for the settlement did not begin at Yalta, where he was a dying man, but dated back to much earlier in the war when, with his often-repeated conviction that 'I can handle Stalin', he failed to discern the deep ideological content of Soviet policy and also deliberately divorced United States political and military objectives. Stalin, who saw war as an extension of politics, was thus at Yalta able to exploit his military victories to the utmost, dividing, confusing and dominating his Allies.

Within two months of Yalta Roosevelt was dead, killed by the staggering responsibilities he had carried for twelve years. His successor, Harry Truman, at first carried on the Grand Design, refusing to allow Eisenhower's victorious troops to take Berlin in spite of Churchill's appeals. But even before Roosevelt's death, 'It was beginning to be feared that a monstrous fraud had been perpetrated at Yalta, with Roosevelt and Churchill as the unwitting dupes.'[1] Before a month had passed after the conference, the Soviet forces in Poland arrested the leaders of the London-aligned underground, and when the coalition government was at last formed in June the Communists held the key ministries of Public Security, Defence and Information. Yet during the summer of 1945, following the German surrender on 7 May, as the Allied Control Council assumed authority in Germany in June, and as arrangements were made for the Potsdam Conference, the personality of Truman began to make itself felt. When he succeeded to the presidency he had known

[1] Robert Sherwood, *Roosevelt and Hopkins* (1948), p. 876.

virtually nothing of the great secret decisions of the war, including Roosevelt's order in 1942 to build the atomic bomb 'as fast as possible'. Yet Truman was a man of strong principles. When Molotov, the Soviet foreign minister, visited him on 23 April, Truman dressed him down for Soviet non-observance of the Yalta decisions on Poland: 'I have never been talked to like that in my life', complained the Russian. It was a portent of things to come as Truman, during the summer of 1945, began to divest himself of Roosevelt's policies — and cabinet members.

Truman's account of the Potsdam Conference shows how far events had moved since Yalta. Of the interminable and often hostile exchanges between the three leaders — Churchill was replaced in mid-conference by Clement Attlee, leader of the victorious Labour Party in the British General Election — Truman remarks in his *Memoirs* that 'on a number of occasions, I felt like blowing the roof off the [Cecilienhof] Palace'. The conference agreed that while the German economy was to be decentralised, Germany was to be treated as an economic unity, and a Council of Foreign Ministers would draft a peace settlement with the vanquished. The Poles, pending this settlement with Germany (which twenty years later was still unsigned) were to be given the boundary of the Oder–western Neisse line — the German territory in question had already been turned over to them by the Russians and its millions of inhabitants driven off to the West.

But perhaps the most pregnant decisions of the conference concerned the Pacific war. On 16 July, the day after his arrival at Potsdam, Truman received a message from Washington: WAR 32887 ... OPERATED ON THIS MORNING. DIAGNOSIS NOT YET COMPLETE BUT RESULTS SEEM SATISFACTORY AND ALREADY EXCEED EXPECTATIONS. ... The first atomic bomb had been exploded that same day at Alamogordo, New Mexico. At the same time he also received Stalin's 'personal reaffirmation' of forthcoming Soviet action against Japan. No reply having been received from Tokyo to the Potsdam Declaration inviting Japan's surrender, Truman, with Churchill's approval, issued orders to use the bomb; by the time Hiroshima was vaporised on 6 August the President was on his way home. A second bomb destroyed Nagasaki on 9 August, the day following the Soviet declaration of war against Japan; Stalin's troops immediately advanced into Manchuria, north China and Korea, where the 38th Parallel was designated the demarcation line between the American and Russian occupation zones. At last, on 14 August, Tokyo accepted the Potsdam Declaration, and later on the same day the 'Son of Heaven' promulgated an Imperial rescript announcing Japan's decision to surrender, which he broadcast to his shattered people the next day (VJ Day). Eighteen days later, on 2 September 1945, General Douglas MacArthur received Japan's formal capitulation in a dramatic ceremony on the decks of the *Missouri* anchored in Tokyo Bay. The Pacific war was ended.

Yet Truman's reflections on his return to Washington from Potsdam show him convinced that while the Axis had been defeated, peace was by no means inevitable. His experiences with the Russians had convinced him that they should not be allowed any voice in the administration of conquered Japan: '. . . the personal meeting with Stalin . . . enabled me to see at first hand what we and the West had to face in the future. . . . It was clear that the Russian foreign policy was based on the conclusion that we were heading for a major depression, and they were already planning to take advantage of our setback.' The war was over, but so was the bizarre shotgun-marriage of the Grand Alliance. With his usual prescience Churchill had code-named the Potsdam Conference, TERMINAL.

THE END OF THE 'GRAND DESIGN'

The eighteen months following the Potsdam Conference are crucial to an understanding of the later evolution of the cold war. During 1945–6 the American national mood was virtually isolationist; the huge US armed forces were swiftly demobilised, and, officially, American foreign policy towards the rest of the world was based on the ideas of cooperation with Russia, the rule of universal law and the United Nations — an extension of the Grand Design, although Truman himself was increasingly suspicious of Soviet policy. In effect there was a policy-vacuum in Washington.

On the other hand the Soviet leaders saw their present military strength as an unprecedented opportunity for the establishment of Communist régimes in a number of former capitalist countries. The power of the Red Army, combined with the total economic, social and political collapse of most of Europe, to say nothing of the chaos in China, had produced a situation of historic advantage for the Communists, an unparalleled vindication of the Marxist-Leninist creed that the bourgeois world-system would collapse after a series of just such frightful collisions as had just occurred. There can be little doubt that Stalin saw the immediate post-war situation as a moment of destiny for the Soviet leadership; it was conceivable that their writ might be advanced to the Atlantic. At the same time the ideological warning was sounded, and, in November 1945, on the twenty-eighth anniversary of the Russian revolution, Molotov warned that 'as long as the roots of fascism and imperialist aggression have not finally been extirpated, our vigilance in regard to possible new violators of peace should not slacken. . . .' And as if preparing the faithful for the very worst eventuality, Stalin, three months later, on 9 February 1946, referred to a possibility of a conflict between capitalism and Communism.

Thus between 1945 and 1948 nearly all the territories under Soviet military occupation, between the 38th Parallel in Korea and the western boundaries of the Soviet zone of Germany, a bare hundred miles from the Rhine, were brought under Moscow's political control. Yugoslavia, where Tito's Communist partisans had won their own war, was a special case as we shall see, and in Czechoslovakia the *coup* was postponed until 1948, but in Poland, Bulgaria, Rumania and Hungary coalition governments with Communist representation eventually succumbed to violence, intimidation and rigged elections under the umbrella of Soviet troops to become Communist-controlled states and, before long, fully-fledged 'people's democracies'. (In Communist theory the class nature of the people's democracy was essentially identical to that of the Soviet state — rule by 'the dictatorship of the working class'.) In the Soviet zone of Germany the creation of the Socialist Unity Party (SED) in April 1946 was followed by the *gleichschaltung* of the Social Democrats (SPD) throughout the zone; in Manchuria Soviet troops turned over Japanese arms to the Chinese Communists while still negotiating for concessions from the Nationalists; and in North Korea an embryo Communist puppet state was in existence by February 1946. As Stalin told Milovan Djilas in Moscow in April 1945: 'This war is not as in the past; whoever occupies a territory also imposes on it his own social system. Everyone imposes his own system as far as his army has power to do so. It cannot be otherwise.'[1] The opening stages of this process, as Stalin's golden horde swept into central Europe in the summer of 1945 to avenge the Wehrmacht's terror in Russia, appeared as a new *Volkerwanderung*. First came the Soviet armoured divisions, 'well disciplined, well armed and trained . . . the columns of guns and lorries, the parachute divisions, motor cyclists, technical units . . .'. They were followed by

[1] M. Djilas, *Conversations with Stalin* (1963), p. 90.

columns of marching soldiers, dirty, tired, clad in ragged uniforms — tens and hundreds of thousands of columns . . . columns of women and girls in military grey-green uniforms, high boots and tight blouses, with long hair greased with goose-fat . . . children, mainly small boys; the *bezprizorni* from burned-out villages and towns. . . . Behind the first spearheads drive the staff; they drive in German luxury cars . . . cars with their secretaries and secretary-girl friends and secretary companions . . . cars with war-booty, cases of china, kilometres of textile materials, fur coats, carpets, silver. . . . Cars of the Agitprop Brigade with broadcasting apparatus and theatrical properties . . . lorries belonging to the Political Commissariat, the staffs and motorised units of the NKVD . . . lorries with tons of Russian delicacies, caviar, sturgeon, salami, hectolitres of vodka and Crimean wine. . . . Behind the staffs more marching columns, without a beginning and without an end . . . finally the rearguard; miles and miles of small light carts drawn by low Cossack horses . . . as the Tartars used to drive centuries ago . . . a flood from the Steppes, spreading across Europe. . . .[1]

But Stalin's ambitions do not only involve those territories under Red Army occupation. There was an active attempt to extend Soviet control beyond this zone. In June 1945 Moscow suggested joint control of the Straits to the Turkish government — a proposal which would have put a Soviet garrison on the Dardanelles; at the same time Turkey was asked to return to Russia the frontier districts of Kars and Ardahan, ceded in 1921. These pressures continued throughout 1946. Across the border in Persia during November 1945 a Communist 'democratic' régime was formed in Azerbaijan, and in March 1946 a shadowy 'Kurdish Republic' was also proclaimed on Persian soil. Only after the most intense Anglo-American diplomatic pressure did Soviet troops withdraw from these regions, leaving the secessionist régimes to collapse at the end of 1946. Outraged by Soviet behaviour in Persia, Truman wrote to Secretary of State James Byrnes in January 1946:

[1] J. Stransky, *East Wind over Prague* (1950), pp. 22–25.

'Unless Russia is faced by an iron fist and strong language another war is in the making.'[1] Most important of all during this period, in March 1946, what the Communist press called 'persecuted democratic citizens' went into action in the Olympus area of Greece; it was the beginning of three years of civil war which ravaged the whole country. Moreover, these events in Persia, Greece and Turkey took place well before the defensive measures of the Truman Doctrine in 1947 and could not possibly be a response to what the Communist propaganda apparatus called 'Western encirclement'.

But gradually American opinion was beginning to see that it could not let Europe and the Middle East fall to the Soviet by default. On 5 March 1946 the voice of Winston Churchill was heard from Westminster College, Fulton, Missouri, while Truman sat next to him on the platform:

A shadow has fallen upon the scenes so lately lighted by the Allied victory. Nobody knows what Soviet Russia and its Communist international organisation intends to do in the immediate future, or what are the limits, if any, to their expansive and proselytising tendencies. I have a strong admiration and regard for the valiant Russian people and for my war-time comrade, Marshal Stalin. There is sympathy and goodwill in Britain — and, I doubt not, here also — towards the peoples of all the Russias, and a resolve to persevere through many differences and rebuffs in establishing lasting friendships. We understand the Russian need to be secure on her Western frontiers from all renewal of German aggression. We welcome her to her rightful place among the leading nations of the world. Above all, we welcome constant, frequent, and growing contacts between the Russian people and our own people on both sides of the Atlantic. It is my duty, however, to place before you certain facts about the present position in Europe.

From Stettin, in the Baltic, to Trieste, in the Adriatic, an iron curtain[2] has descended across the continent. Behind

[1] Harry S. Truman, *Year of Decisions, 1945* (1955), p. 492.

[2] Churchill had already referred to 'an iron curtain' drawn down on the Russian front in a message to Truman on 12 May 1945. See *Triumph and Tragedy* (1954), pp. 498–9.

that line all the capitals of the ancient states of central and eastern Europe — Warsaw, Berlin, Prague, Vienna, Buda-pest, Belgrade, Bucharest and Sofia. All these famous cities, and the populations around them, lie in the Soviet sphere, and all are subject in one form or another, not only to Soviet influence, but to a very high and increasing measure of control from Moscow. Athens alone, with its immortal glories, is free to decide its future at an election under British, American and French observation. The Russian-dominated Polish government has been encouraged to make enormous and wrongful inroads upon Germany, and mass expulsions of millions of Germans on a scale grievous and undreamed of are now taking place. The Communist parties, which were very small in those eastern states of Europe, have been raised to pre-eminence and power far beyond their numbers, and are seeking everywhere to obtain totalitarian control. Police governments are prevail-ing in nearly every case, and so far, except in Czechoslovakia, there is no true democracy. Turkey and Persia are both profoundly alarmed and disturbed at the claims which are being made upon them and at the pressure being exerted by the Moscow government. An attempt is being made by the Russians in Berlin to build up a quasi-Communist party in their zone of occupied Germany by showing special favours to groups of Left-wing German leaders.

At the end of the fighting last June, the American and British armies withdrew westwards, in accordance with an earlier agreement, to a depth at some points of 150 miles on a front of nearly 400 miles, to allow the Russians to occupy this vast expanse of territory which the Western democracies had conquered. If, now, the Soviet government tries, by separate action, to build up a pro-Communist Germany in their areas, this will cause new serious diffi-culties in the British and American zones, and will give the defeated Germans the power of putting themselves up to auction between the Soviets and the Western democracies. Whatever conclusions may be drawn from these facts — and facts they are — this is certainly not the liberated Europe we fought to build up. Nor is it one which contains the essentials of permanent peace. . . .[1]

[1] *Select Documents on Germany and the Question of Berlin, 1944–1961* (1961), pp. 64–65.

As Churchill rightly saw, it was Germany that lay at the heart of the developing conflict; the Russians had violated the Potsdam agreements and had sealed off their zone, economically as well as politically, so that the Anglo-Americans were both supplying reparations to the USSR from their zones while yet pouring in money in an attempt to set up a viable German economy. Such a state of affairs was manifestly ridiculous, and, looking back, we can see that the foundations of the present West German state were laid in the summer of 1946. First, in May, reparations were suspended from the American zone, and then in July the Anglo-Americans agreed on a complete economic fusion of their zones; Bizonia came into operation in January 1947. Then, in another reversal of US policy, Byrnes, in a famous speech at Stuttgart in September, declared that 'as long as there is an occupation army in Germany, American forces will be part of that army'.

At the same time, there was a growing realisation in Washington that US policy stood at a historic crossroads. Mutual confidence between Truman and Byrnes was lacking; Truman complains in his *Memoirs* that the war-time authority Byrnes had enjoyed under Roosevelt had had 'an extraordinary influence' on him, leading him to the delusion he could conduct policy without reference to the President. Moreover, in 1944, Byrnes had hoped to win the Democratic party vice-presidential nomination, which, of course, had been won by Truman. In any case, Byrnes's legalistic approach was ill-suited to foreign affairs and in January 1947, after negotiating the Italian and the Axis–satellite peace treaties, he was replaced by General George Marshall. Already Henry Wallace, the leading advocate inside Truman's cabinet of the soft line towards Moscow, had been dismissed the previous September. Yet the great crisis which committed the United States to a new global balance of power did not arise over Germany, as many had forecast. In February 1947, as Britain faced economic disintegration after a crippling series of blizzards, the Attlee Government told Washington that it could not continue economic and military assistance to Greece and Turkey; unless the United States acted, the collapse of Western Eurasia seemed imminent.[1]

1947: THE STRUGGLE BETWEEN ROME AND CARTHAGE?

Ernest Bevin's note to the US government on 21 February, which announced that Britain could no longer continue assistance to Greece and Turkey, precipitated a heroic period of policy-making in Washington. After consultations with the three other countries involved, on 12 March 1947 Truman presented a Bill to Congress asking for $400 million for economic and military aid to Greece and Turkey. The speech, which outlined the new American programme in ideological as well as economic terms, appealed to American idealism as well as self-interest; the new policy immediately became known as the Truman Doctrine:

> ... I believe that it must be the policy of the United States to support free peoples who are resisting attempted subjugation by armed minorities or by outside pressures. I believe that we must assist free peoples to work out their own destinies in their own way. I believe that our help should be primarily through economic and financial aid which is essential to economic stability and orderly political progress. ...
> Our way of life is based on the will of the majority, and is distinguished by free institutions, representative government, free elections ... The second way of life is based upon the will of a minority forcibly imposed upon the majority. It relies upon terror and oppression ... The free peoples of the world look to us for support in maintaining their

[1] For a more detailed analysis of the economic problems and policies of the post-war period, see Harrison, *The Framework of Economic Activity* (1967), in this series.

B

freedom . . . If we falter in our leadership, we may endanger
the peace of the world — and we shall surely endanger the
welfare of our nation. . . .[1]

But it was recognised by the administration that aid to
Greece and Turkey was not enough; the entire continent
would have to be rehabilitated with US aid, for in the weeks
following the promulgation of the Truman Doctrine, Western Europe still seemed on the verge of economic collapse.
'What is Europe now?' asked Winston Churchill in May
1947. 'It is a rubble heap, a charnel house, a breeding
ground of pestilence and hate. . . .' After intensive activity
behind the scenes, on 8 May, Under-Secretary of State
Dean Acheson stated that US aid would have to be con-
centrated where it would be most effective in building
economic and political stability. Acheson went on: 'The
achievement of a co-ordinated European economy remains
a fundamental objective of our foreign policy.'

This was a trial balloon for Secretary Marshall's speech
at Harvard on 5 June. Marshall remarked on this famous
occasion that the rehabilitation of Europe would take much
longer than anyone had foreseen; and that the United
States should provide a cure rather than a palliative:

Our policy is directed not against any country or doctrine
but against hunger, poverty, desperation and chaos. Its
purpose should be revival of a working economy. . . . Any
government that is willing to assist in the task of recovery
will find full co-operation . . . on the part of the United
States Government. . . . The initiative, I think, must come
from Europe. . . .

When Ernest Bevin first heard of the speech he fell out of
bed and went immediately to his office to take up the offer,
for the British Foreign Minister recognised instantly that
here was the proposal that could save Western Europe.
When Bevin and Molotov met in Paris later in the month

[1] H. S. Truman, *Memoirs*, vol ii, *Years of Trial and Hope* (1956),
pp. 111–12.

it soon became clear that the British and the French were eager to accept the plan on a continental basis, while Molotov insisted that each country should separately administer its Marshall Aid. The Marshall Plan thus became a Western European plan, and the Communists were outmanœuvred, appearing to be ranged on the side of 'hunger, poverty, desperation and chaos'. By the following April the 'European Recovery Programme', disbursing 17 billion dollars, had been approved by Congress, and in the associated US Economic Co-operation Administration and the Organisation for European Economic Co-operation we can not only see the means of saving Western Europe from the ravages of war but the beginnings of the later European Economic Community.

Yet in these hectic months of 1947 two more developments must be noted. If the Truman Doctrine and the Marshall Plan provided a material framework of Western recovery, so the fertile mind of George Kennan, a veteran diplomat and now head of the State Department's Policy Planning Staff, provided an intellectual framework for the new American (and Western) foreign policy. Kennan's argument, which appeared in the July 1947 issue of *Foreign Affairs* as 'The Sources of Soviet Conduct' by 'Mr. X', had immense influence at the time and was reprinted for a wider audience in *Life*. He showed how the basic antagonism of the Soviet Union 'will be with us, whether in the foreground or the background, until the internal nature of Soviet power is changed. . . . In these circumstances it is clear than the main element of any United States policy towards the Soviet Union must be that of a long-term, patient but firm and vigilant containment of Russian expansive tendencies.' The Moscow régime might eventually mellow: in the meantime the United States could do much to complement its political counter-measures by displaying spiritual vitality and confidence both to its allies and to the Communists. In effect, the containment policy meant that there could be no decisive violent response by the United States to the Soviet threat, as there had been to the Axis bid for world domination; the place of the Truman Doctrine and the Marshall Plan in such a policy may be easily seen, and also the later evolution of the North Atlantic Treaty and other regional alliances. Indeed, in one way or another, the pragmatic ideas of the containment thesis have permeated Western foreign policy ever since 1947 as the most effective answer, short of war or capitulation, to the spectrum of widely differing crises originating in the developing conflict between East and West.

But the Communist answer to the Truman decisions of 1947 imposed enormous stresses on the emerging containment policy. On 5 October 1947, *Pravda* revealed that a conference in Poland of delegates from the Communist parties of nine European countries had established a Communist Information Bureau — a successor to the Comintern, dissolved in 1943. The meeting had been attended by A. A. Zhdanov and G. M. Malenkov, as senior delegates from Moscow, and delegates from France and Italy as well as from the USSR and the east European satellites had been present.

The Cominform's declaration reaffirmed the faith of the participating parties in the Soviet leadership, called for the defeat of the Marshall Plan, 'a European branch of the general world plan of political expansion being realised by the US', and firmly divided the world into the US-led imperialist camp, and the peace-loving camp headed by the USSR. The world Communist Parties were to 'place themselves in the vanguard of the opposition against the imperialistic plans of expansion. . . .'

The formation of the Cominform was therefore a declaration of direct political warfare against the West and its consequences permeated the cold war until the formal adoption of Khrushchev's new 'coexistence' strategy in 1956. Within a few weeks of the Cominform declaration,

Communist Parties in Western Europe moved into militant opposition to their national governments, and in France and Italy there were Communist-led general strikes, deploying millions of workers and openly revolutionary in aim. The entire European scene became charged with suspense and fear. A few months previously, in June 1947, James Forrestal had asked Truman in a cabinet meeting what the US would do if there were a Russian *démarche* accompanied by *coups* in France and Italy. Truman's reply was that 'he was afraid the answer would have to be found in history — of the struggle between the Romans and Carthage, between Athens and Sparta, between Alexander the Great and Persia, between France and England, between England and Germany. He *hoped* the present situation would not have to be answered the same way. . . .'[1] But by the winter of 1947-8 it appeared as if the answer had already been found — in the present, rather than 'in history'.

NATO: 'AN ATTACK AGAINST ONE . . . AN ATTACK AGAINST ALL . . .'

The Cominform's declaration made it clear as never before that the aim of the Soviet leaders was to fight and destroy the political systems of the West. But the Communist offensive was not confined to Europe. In accordance with the classic Marxist–Leninist dictum that imperialism could be decisively weakened by detaching its colonial dependencies, armed uprisings were staged during 1948 by the Communist parties in south-east Asia, uprisings which were in all probability co-ordinated during the Communist-sponsored South-east Asian Youth Conference at Calcutta in February of that year.

By June 1948 the Malayan Communist Party was in action against the British colonial government, and in the

[1] Walter Millis and E. S. Duffield (ed.), *The Forrestal Diaries* (1951), p. 280.

Philippines the Communist-led Huks were also attempting to overthrow the newly-independent Manila régime. There were also abortive uprisings against the nationalist administrations in Burma and Indonesia, events that showed that Stalin had completely failed to realise the power of nationalism in the former colonial territories. In Malaya the Communists were eventually defeated by the mobilisation of this emergent nationalism, and in the Philippines by agrarian reform. Only in Indo-China, where the French refused to make any effective concessions to anti-colonial sentiment, did the guerrillas of Ho Chi Minh, in action since 1946, make any headway. We shall see how much greater flexibility Soviet policy acquired in the 'third world' during the 1950s, yet even as late as 1953 the *Large Soviet Encyclopaedia* was describing Gandhi as 'an agent of British imperialism'.

Serious as these Asian uprisings were at first, throughout 1948–9 it was Europe which lay at the centre of the conflict. Czechoslovakia was Stalin's next conquest. In February 1948, after intense pressure by the Communist 'workers' militia' and 'action committees', backed by the threat of civil war, against a democratic government, President Beneš capitulated and agreed to the formation of a Communist government in Prague. Within a few weeks Jan Masaryk, the Foreign Minister, was found dead, and the *coup* had become a Communist textbook example of the 'revolution from above'. Meanwhile, Tito was being excommunicated by the Cominform, which, when it met for the second time in June 1948, announced that Yugoslavia had been expelled for various doctrinal reasons, including that of bourgeois nationalism. In reality the Yugoslavs had resisted Stalin's pressure to obtain key privileges in the state and party apparatus, as he had done in other satellite countries. Within weeks 'the Tito clique' were being denounced as imperialist agents, and it seemed as if at any moment a revolt or satellite-sponsored invasion might be launched against the Belgrade government, which later publicly claimed that Stalin's policy was aimed at 'the subjection of Yugoslavia'. By November 1949, after a third Cominform meeting in Hungary, the Tito clique was accused of having 'definitely passed from bourgeois nationalism to fascism' — Tito was thus bracketed with Franco and Salazar. This Cominform conference marked the opening of Stalin's great assize of Communist leaders in Eastern Europe — Rajk in Hungary, Kostov in Bulgaria, Slansky in Czechoslovakia, and Xoxe in Albania — all of whom were given show-trials and executed as Titoists and agents of the Anglo-American intelligence services.

But it was over Berlin and Germany during the months that led to the signing of the North Atlantic Treaty in April 1949 that the great confrontation of this phase of the cold war took place. And indeed, because of the immense resources of an united Germany, and the significance of a free West Berlin deep in Communist territory, the country had always been at the centre of the cold war. So great are the stakes here, that one false move could precipitate instant war: in the 1960s, as in 1948, this was the one campaign of the cold war that neither side could lose. Between 1945 and 1949 Soviet policy was aimed at the collapse of the Western occupations zones — and the establishment of a unified, Communist-controlled Germany. But as the United States agreed to extend Marshall Aid to Bizonia during 1947-8, as the West agreed in principle to the formation of a West German Federal Republic, and as the United Kingdom, France and Benelux signed the Brussels Treaty in March 1948 it was obvious that the Allies were slowly perfecting their defences.

The weakest point in the Western position lay in Berlin, where there existed a special four-power régime, physically separated from West Germany by a hundred miles of the Soviet-controlled territory. (The allied occupation zones of defeated Germany, together with the isolated Berlin enclave, had their origin in a British cabinet committee plan of 1943.) But in Berlin, as in West Germany, Allied rights were indisputable. The Allies were there by right of conquest, the basis of their presence in Berlin to this day. In June 1948 the Western Allies announced a currency reform in their zones of Germany and of West Berlin; and at 6 a.m., 24 June 1948, after months of harassment, all rail and road routes to Berlin from the West were cut by the Russians on the grounds of 'technical difficulties'. The results of a Western withdrawal would have been incalculable. On Truman's insistence the USAF soon organised an airlift into the city, an immense operation, to which the RAF contributed one-third of the effort, and which eventually delivered, in nearly 300,000 flights, over two million tons of supplies. The Russians had obviously calculated that the airlift was impossible and, when it had begun, that winter would stop the endless flow of aircraft. Interference with Allied aircraft would have been too dangerous; and when at last the blockade was lifted on 12 May 1949, after secret negotiations, the Russians admitted a spectacular defeat. The courage, resolution and ingenuity[1] shown by the Allied governments, the aircrews, and the Berliners have never been forgotten; and when Soviet policy moved on through 'neutralisation' proposals to Khrushchev's 'two Germanies' offensive at the end of the 1950s, the memory of the airlift was one of the chief reasons why any withdrawal from Berlin was still regarded as unthinkable.

[1] 'A few days after Clay and I returned to Berlin from Washington, Clay telephoned [General] LeMay [USAF] in Frankfurt. Clay asked: "Have you any planes there that can carry coal?"

"Carry what?" asked LeMay.

"Coal", repeated Clay.

"We must have a bad phone connection", said LeMay. "It sounds as if you are asking if we have planes for carrying coal."

"Yes, that's what I said — coal."

Rallying quickly, LeMay said stoutly, "The Air Force can deliver anything ... " ' (Robert Murphy, *Diplomat Among Warriors* (1964), p. 389).

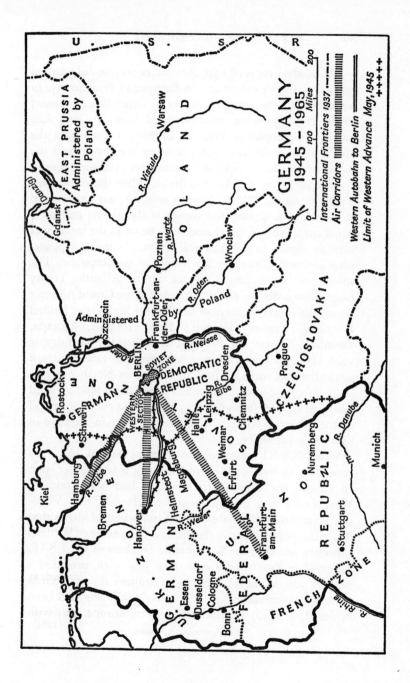

Yet, as the events of 1948 showed, economic aid was not enough to restore confidence in Europe; as Truman says in his *Memoirs*, 'the constant threat of unpredictable Soviet moves resulted in an atmosphere of insecurity and fear among the peoples of Western Europe.' Even before the airlift, secret talks had begun between the British and the Americans with a view to creating an Atlantic security system, including the United States. After the most complex discussions, a North Atlantic security pact was evolved in Washington during the winter of the airlift; and on 4 April 1949 Truman stood next to Acheson as the treaty was fittingly signed in the American capital — the first peacetime military alliance in the history of the Republic. The subsequent development of the North Atlantic Treaty Organisation does not belong here[1]; but the Grand Alliance which the representatives of the United States, the United Kingdom, France, Benelux, Italy, Iceland, Canada, Denmark, Norway and Portugal signed has the most simple vital clause: 'The Parties agree that an armed attack against one or more of them in Europe or North America shall be considered an attack against them all. . . .' And whatever its later imperfections, NATO has ever since stood at the heart of Western diplomacy — even in its time of troubles in the 1960s.

When NATO came into force on 24 August 1949, the economic recovery of Western Europe was well under way. In Greece the Communist partisans had been crushed, West Berlin had been successfully defended, and Yugoslavia was still independent. Most important of all, in that American power was still the ultimate guarantee of Western collective security, the B-29 atomic bombers of the USAF, stationed in East Anglia ever since July 1948, provided a decisive sanction against the Soviet military threat. Thanks to American resolution, a new balance of power had been achieved, a world restored in Western Europe. But with

[1] See Appendix A, below.

one of those great historical ironies with which the cold war abounds, no sooner had the North Atlantic Treaty been ratified, than at the end of August an US patrol aircraft over the Pacific collected a radio-active air sample; it was the fall-out from 'Joe One'. The Soviets had exploded an atomic bomb three years ahead of the schedule assigned to them by the Americans; on 23 September 1949 Truman laconically announced that 'We have evidence that within recent weeks an atomic explosion occurred in the USSR'. A week later, on 1 October 1949, the Chinese People's Republic was proclaimed in Peking. The line would be held inviolate in Europe, but in the Far East a completely new phase of the cold war had begun.

2 1949-1953
Thunder out of China

THE LONG MARCH

As we have seen, throughout the 1945-9 period it was in Europe and the Middle East where, in Marxist jargon, 'the struggle on the main front' was waged. Underlying all the American counter-measures against Stalin's forward policy was the fear that a third world war might develop out of the unprecedented peace-time tensions raised by the cold war. At the same time it was expected that if the worst came, it would begin with a Soviet invasion of Western Europe, a move which would be answered by an annihilating atomic counter-blow against Russian cities and industrial centres by the US Strategic Air Command. Barely a year after the formation of NATO Stalin did attempt to extend his empire by military means, but the blow fell not in the West, but in remote Korea. Moreover, the war which went on in Korea for three years, after the invasion of South Korea by the northern régime in June 1950, did not develop into the total war that had been foreseen by Western strategists; instead, a limited war, a conflict for which the Western allies were both militarily and politically ill-prepared, dragged on until it had changed the entire defence posture of the United States and its allies.

The Korean War was instigated by Moscow. Yet within a few months of June 1950 the forces of Communist China, as we shall see, crossed the Yalu into Korea, and the war became essentially a trial of strength between the US and the Peking régime. It was only during the long-drawn-out months of the Korean War that the full significance of the

Chinese Communist seizure of power became recognised in the West. Yet the Chinese revolution had begun as long ago as 1911; and in view not only of the Korean War and its aftermath but of the later Sino-Soviet dispute it is necessary here to look briefly at the rise of the Chinese Communist Party (CCP) and its famous leader, Mao Tse-tung.[1]

Historically, of course, the roots of the Chinese Revolution, like those of the Russian Revolution, lie in the events of the mid-nineteenth century. In China the first significant event is the Opium War of 1839–42 — the initial impact of the West upon the moribund Celestial Empire in the shape of British merchant adventurers determined to carve out lucrative commercial concessions. Then, in 1911, after decades of Western domination, began the revolution which overthrew the Manchus, inspired by the nationalist ideals of Dr. Sun Yat-sen, who wished to modernise China on Western lines; but for the next seventeen years the country was riven between rival war lords, Dr Sun Yat-sen's 'National People's Party,' the Kuomintang (KMT), created in 1912, which in exile on Formosa still venerates its founder's memory with divine honours, and the Chinese Communist Party (CCP), formed in 1921. Between 1924 and 1927 a 'revolutionary situation' developed in China which Moscow hoped to turn into its advantage; Stalin expected to mobilise the masses in the cities against the bankers, landlords and foreign interests in a revolution led by the KMT (Kuomintang), a revolution which would be taken over by the CCP.

In 1925 Dr. Sun Yat-sen died and was succeeded by his protégé, General Chiang Kai-shek, who had already visited Russia and flirted with the Comintern. Stalin was confident of victory, and a period of KMT–CCP collaboration begun. In April 1927 Stalin boasted to Party cadres in Moscow that the KMT would be 'squeezed out like a lemon and

[1] The subject will be treated at greater length in another essay in this series.

then thrown away'.[1] But a few days later on 12 April 1927 Chiang struck against the Communists in Shanghai in a purge of awesome proportions, a purge commemorated in André Malraux's novel *La Condition humaine* (1933). By the end of the year the Communists throughout China had been crushed as an effective force by Chiang and his warlord allies, and the period of KMT–CCP collaboration was over. The next year the victorious Chiang became head of the internationally-recognised National Government of China, while the Communists were now hunted bandits. In the remote hills of Kiangsi, Mao Tse-tung and a few followers survived to create a new Communist movement based on agrarian revolution and guerrilla warfare, rather than on the city-based strategy of Marxist orthodoxy favoured by Moscow. And Mao was, moreover, as emphatic in his anti-foreign nationalism as Chiang or Sun Yat-sen. In the face of immense hardships Mao survived a series of 'extermination' campaigns launched by Chiang in the early 1930s, but in 1934 the KMT pressure became so great that the Communists began their heroic Long March of 5,000 miles from south-east China to the north-west; it was during the Long March, in January 1935, that Mao Tse-tung assumed effective control of the CCP when he was appointed to the newly created post of Chairman of the Politburo and since then the Party's history is inextricably linked with Mao's own story.

Blockaded by the KMT in his Shensi headquarters of Yenan after the end of the Long March in the summer of 1935, Mao codified his theories of peasant guerrilla warfare in a series of classic studies which have since become blue-prints of anti-colonial revolt: 'Mao elaborated his ideas on the basis of Chinese experience, but the factors that under-lay these theories — agrarian discontent, impatience with existing conditions, national solidarity in the face of the West — are to a considerable extent present in many Asian,

[1] R. North, *Moscow and the Chinese Communists* (1953), p. 96.

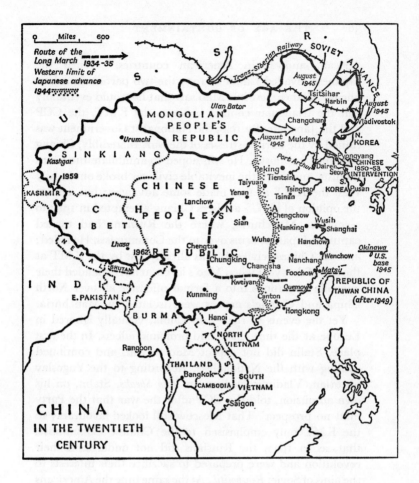

CHINA
IN THE TWENTIETH
CENTURY

African, and Latin American countries.'[1] When the
Japanese invaded China in 1937 the two parties signed an
uneasy alliance; few but Mao saw that he would eventually
win the triangular conflict between the KMT, the CCP
and the Japanese. By 1945 the Nationalist Government was
ruined by the terrible stresses of the war. Incredibly, Chiang
remained optimistic. He still hoped to annihilate the Communists, and when the inevitable civil war broke out in July
1946 the KMT at first made some advances; but against
the opinion of his US advisers Chiang attempted in 1947 to
reconquer Manchuria, where the Russians had turned
captured Japanese arms over to the Communists. He failed;
and the Chinese civil war was already lost by the KMT at
the end of that year when Mao's forces at last expanded their
guerrilla operations into a formal offensive all over North
China and Chiang's armies were isolated in Manchuria.

Yet the events of 1946–7 in China, virtually ignored in
Europe at the time, have had profound effects. In the first
place, Stalin did not expect Mao to win, and continued
dealing with the Nationalists. According to the Yugoslav
historian, Vladimir Dedijer, in *Tito Speaks*, Stalin, on his
own admission, told the CCP after the war that the Party
'had no prospect'. That Moscow still looked favourably to
the KMT only emphasised to the Chinese Communists
that, as in 1927, the Russians did not understand their
revolution and were prepared to sacrifice their interests to
the aims of Soviet *Realpolitik*. At the same time the Americans
also doubted the competence of their allies; General
Marshall arrived in China in December 1945 with instruc-
tions from Truman to reconcile the KMT and the CCP. It
was an impossible task, and when Marshall left China for
ever in January 1947 he acknowledged failure. Yet his year
of misconceived mediation had been put to good use by the
Communists, when they were in a militarily disadvan-
tageous position immediately following the end of the

[1] Stuart R. Schram, *The Political Thought of Mao Tse-tung* (1963), p. 61.

Pacific war; by the end of 1947 Mao at last knew that his war was won. Throughout 1948 and 1949 the Communists rolled back the shattered Kuomintang armies from Manchuria across the Yangtse until Chiang sought refuge in Formosa and by October 1949 virtually the whole of the mainland was under Communist control. The 'Mandate of Heaven' had thus passed from Chiang to Mao. And within a year the 'New China' would be engaged in open warfare with the United States — on the hills of Korea.

KOREA: WAR WITHOUT VICTORY

When the massed armies of Communist China crossed the Yalu in October 1950 to enter the Korean War, fighting had already been going on for four months in what had been known for centuries as the 'Land of the Morning Calm'. The development of the war in Korea has a special importance in the history of the cold war, for it is the only instance — at the time of writing — in which the Communists have resorted to direct conventional military aggression. And the manœuvres of the great powers involved to limit the savage fighting to Korea are relevant in answering the question: how does the West best defend its interests in an age when general war will result in the atomic holocaust?

But in any case, no one foresaw in 1947 that it would be in Korea that Stalin's great offensive against the West would come to its climax. The country was partitioned between the Russians and the Americans in 1945 as a military arrangement to facilitate the Japanese surrender, and the demarcation line of the 38th Parallel soon became the iron curtain in the Far East. By 1948 two rival régimes, each claiming sovereignty over the whole country, had been established, the Republic of Korea in the south, and in the north the Democratic People's Republic of Korea. The southern régime was established after UN-supervised

elections; but that in the Soviet zone was a creation of the
Russian occupation authorities. In June 1949 US occupation
troops were withdrawn from South Korea, and both General
Douglas MacArthur, who had ruled Japan in vice-regal
style as the Supreme Commander for the Allies since 1945,
and the Administration in Washington had decided that
South Korea lay outside the US Pacific defence-perimeter,
a fact which Acheson publicly acknowledged in January
1950. Budgetary economies also contributed to the US
withdrawal.

With Soviet expansionist adventures blocked in Europe
by NATO, the withdrawal from South Korea unfortunately
created a certain ambiguity in American policy; it seems
likely that Moscow calculated that the United States *might*
tolerate a take-over in South Korea, a country in a remoter
sector of the cold war. Ample evidence exists of a North
Korean Army build-up during the winter of 1949–50; and
on 25 June 1950 seven North Korean infantry divisions and
an armoured division struck across the 38th Parallel. The
invaders were equipped with Soviet arms, including T-34
tanks and Yak fighters; Soviet instructors advised the
higher echelons of the North Korean Army; that the invasion
could have been launched without Moscow's sanction is
inconceivable. Truman's historic response to this brazen
aggression is described in his *Memoirs* as 'the toughest
decision' of his presidency. Air and naval assistance was
immediately given to the Republic of Korea (ROK); and
following this action the UN Security Council, free to act
for once owing to the absence of the Soviet delegate and his
veto which had paralysed the Council ever since 1945,
recommended to UN members that they furnish aid to
South Korea 'to repel the armed attack'. Eventually,
fifteen UN members sent forces to Korea to serve in the UN
Command, although of course the basis of the resistance to
the Communist armies was American power.

Within a week of the invasion Truman had ordered

MacArthur to send in US ground troops from Japan. As the
UN forces were pushed back to the Pusan perimeter in
south-east Korea — many prophesied an evacuation —
MacArthur (designated the first UN Commander) planned
and executed the Napoleonic manœuvre of the Inchon
landing on 15 September 1950; the old soldier placed a
Marine division two hundred miles behind the enemy's lines.
The North Korean Army disintegrated, and the UN General
Assembly voted for a 'united, independent and democratic
Korea' — which could only come about by a US advance
to the Manchurian border. Yet the drive to Yalu, which got
under way in October 1950, was an abandonment of
containment — it aimed at the 'liberation' of a Communist
satellite. Direct Soviet intervention to save the North Korean
régime might well have precipitated general war; it was left
to Communist China to salvage the Pyongyang government. In mid-October the first of 350,000 men of the Chinese
Communist Forces (CCF) crossed the Yalu; in late November MacArthur's final 'Home by Christmas' offensive to the
Yalu was smashed on the Chongchon River by the Chinese,
who then moved south to the 38th Parallel. When Truman
and Attlee, meeting in Washington in December 1950,
decided to abandon the aim of uniting Korea, but to defend
the 38th Parallel, MacArthur protested that the conflict
should be carried to the 'privileged sanctuary' of Manchuria
to win the war.

The next few months were crucial as the battlefront see-
sawed up and down the peninsula. In early 1951, reinforced
US divisions, with a strong British contingent, held the
CCF (Chinese Communist Forces) south of the 38th
Parallel while inflicting huge casualties. When MacArthur
continued his public protests ('There is no substitute for
victory. . . .') Truman, on 11 April 1951, dismissed his
overmighty subject and outlined his policy as one of fighting
a limited war in Korea, so as to avoid a third world war.
Yet on his return to the United States, MacArthur was

given a Roman triumph in New York. But first he had outlined his views on the Korean War to a joint session of Congress on 19 April, after receiving a welcome in the nation's capital almost unsurpassed in its history:

Mr. President [of the Senate], Mr. Speaker, distinguished members of Congress. . . . I do not stand here for any partisan cause, for the issues are fundamental and reach quite beyond the realm of partisan consideration. They must be resolved on the highest plane of national interest if our course is to prove sound and our future protected. . . . I address you with neither rancour nor bitterness in the fading twilight of my life but with one purpose, to serve my country. . . .

Our victory [in Korea] was complete and our objectives within reach when Red China intervened with numerically superior ground forces. . . . While no man in his right mind would advocate sending our ground forces into continental China, and such was never given thought, the new situation did urgently demand a drastic revision of strategic planning if our political aim was to defeat this enemy as we had defeated the old. . . .

(1) The intensification of the economic blockade of China.

(2) The imposition of a naval blockade against the China coast.

(3) Removal of restrictions on air reconnaissance of China's coastal areas and of Manchuria.

(4) Removal of restrictions on the forces of the Republic of China on Formosa with logistical support to contribute to their effective operations against the Chinese mainland. . . .

It has been said [MacArthur went on] in effect that I was a war-monger. Nothing could be further from the truth. I know war as few other men living know it, and nothing, to me, is more revolting. I have long advocated its complete abolition, as its very destructiveness on both friend and foe has rendered it useless as a means of settling international disputes. . . . But once war is forced upon us, there is no other alternative than to apply every available means to bring it to a swift end. . . . War's very object is victory, not prolonged indecision. In war there is no substitute for victory. There are some who, for varying reasons, would appease Red China. They are blind to history's clear lesson, for history teaches, with unmistakable emphasis, that appeasement but begets new and bloodier war. It points to no single instance where this end has justified that means. . . . Like blackmail, it lays the basis for new and successively greater demands until, as in blackmail, violence becomes the only other alternative. Why, my soldiers asked of me, surrender military advantage to an enemy in the field? I could not answer. . . .[1]

MacArthur's attack on the Truman administration's concept of limited war in Korea was followed by a historic Congressional investigation, by the Senate Foreign Relations and Armed Services committees, into the General's dismissal, the Korean War, and indeed the whole basis of American foreign policy. To MacArthur's charge that the Truman administration had 'no policy . . . nothing . . . no plan or anything,' General George Marshall, the Defence Secretary, outlined the essence of the containment policy in words that are as apposite today as they were in 1951:

There can be, I think, no quick and decisive solution to the global struggle short of resorting to another world war. The cost of such a conflict is beyond calculation. It is therefore our policy to contain Communist aggression in different fashions in different areas without resorting to total war. . . . The application of this policy has not always been easy or popular. . . .[2]

Marshall was followed by General Bradley, Chairman of the Joint Chiefs of Staff, who deflated MacArthur's strategy of total victory in Korea by reminding his listeners of the classical approach that the most dangerous enemy was the strongest enemy:

The Joint Chiefs of Staff, in view of their global responsibilities and their perspective with respect to the world-wide strategic situation, are in a better position than is any single

---

[1] The full text of this address is quoted in Senate *MacArthur Hearings* (1951), pp. 3553–8.
[2] Ibid., p. 366.

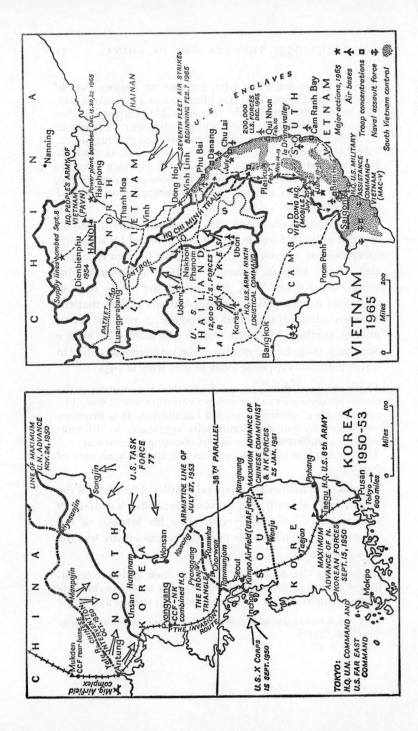

KOREA 1950-53

MAXIMUM ADVANCE OF
CHINESE COMMUNIST
& NK FORCES
25 JAN. 1951

LINE OF MAXIMUM
U.N. ADVANCE
NOV. 24, 1950

U.S. TASK
FORCE 77

ARMISTICE LINE OF
JULY 27, 1953

38TH PARALLEL

MAXIMUM ADVANCE OF N.
KOREAN FORCES
SEPT. 15, 1950

U.S. X CORPS
15 SEPT. 1950

NORTH KOREA

SOUTH KOREA

CHINA

Mukden
CCF rear base
CHINA INTERVENES
OCT. 1950
Antung
Mig Airfield complex
Manpojin
Chinton
Yalu River
Hyesanjin
Songjin
Unsan
Hungnam
Wonsan
Kosong
Pyongyang
CCF-NK
combined H.Q.
Kaesong
Pyonggang
Kumwha
THE IRON
TRIANGLE
Chorwon
Panmunjom
Seoul
Inchon
Kimpo Airfield (USAF jets)
"THE INVASION
ROUTE"
Kangnung
Wonju
Taejon
Taegu H.Q. U.S. 8th ARMY
Pohang
Pusan
Mokpo
Tokyo→
600 miles

TOKYO:
H.Q. U.N. COMMAND AND
U.S. FAR EAST
COMMAND

0   100
Miles

VIETNAM
1965

ENCLAVES

CHINA

Nanning

HAINAN

NORTH VIETNAM

H.Q. PEOPLES ARMY OF
VIETNAM (PAVN)

Supply lines bombed Sept. 8

Dienbienphu
1954

Luangprabang

PATHET LAO

LAOS

HO CHI MINH TRAIL

Power plant bombed Dec. 15, 20, 22 1965

Haiphong

Thanh Hoa

Vinh

HANOI

CONTROL

Dong Hoi
Vinh Linh

SEVENTH FLEET AIR STRIKES
BEGINNING FEB. 7 1965

Phu Bai
Danang
Chu Lai
July 3

la Drang valley
Nov. 14-19

Feb. 10

Qui Nhon

200,000
U.S. FORCES
DEC. 1965

SOUTH VIETNAM

Cam Ranh Bay

Pleiku
Feb. 6, Nov. 14-9

VIETCONG H.Q.
(MOBILE)

July 2017

CAMBODIA

June 10-13

Bien Hoa

H.Q. U.S. MILITARY
ASSISTANCE
COMMAND—
VIETNAM
(MAC-V)

Saigon

THAILAND

Udon

Nakhon
Phanom

12,000 U.S. FORCES

U.S. AIR STRIKES

Ubon

Korat

H.Q. U.S. ARMY NINTH
LOGISTICAL COMMAND

Bangkok

Phnom Penh

0   200
Miles

★ Major actions, 1965   ✈ Air bases
□ Troop concentrations   ✲ Naval assault force

▨ South Vietnam control

theatre commander to assess the risks of general war. Moreover the Joint Chiefs of Staff are best able to judge our own military resources with which to meet that risk. . . . From a global viewpoint . . . our military mission is to support a policy preventing Communism from gaining the manpower, the resources, the raw material and in the industrial capacity essential to world domination. If Soviet Russia ever controls the Eurasian land mass, then the Soviet-satellite imperialism may have the broad base upon which to build the military power to rule the world. . . . Korea, in spite of the importance of the engagement, must be looked upon with proper perspective. It is just one engagement, just one phase of the battle. . . . As long as we keep the conflict within its present scope, we are holding to a mini-mum the force we must commit and tie down. . . . We have recommended against enlarging the war. . . . Red China is not the powerful nation seeking to dominate the world. Frankly, in the opinion of the Joint Chiefs of Staff the [MacArthur] strategy would involve us in the wrong war, at the wrong place, at the wrong time, and with the wrong enemy. . . .[1]

Yet the drama was not ended with the uproar surround-ing MacArthur's recall. Two further mass CCF offensives, aimed at the conquest of South Korea, in April and May 1951 were smashed by US firepower in a spectacular trial of strength around the Parallel, a victory which we see in retrospect marked the beginning of the end for Stalin's great offensive against the West. Defeated on the battlefield, the Communists sued for peace on the basis of the *status quo*, and in July armistice negotiations began at Kaesong, being later transferred to Panmunjom. Bitter fighting still went on at the main line of resistance slightly north of the Parallel, as at Panmunjom the delegations argued interminably over the armistice terms,[2] and over north-west Korea, where massed formations of Russian-built MIG jet-fighters based

[1] Ibid., pp. 730–2.
[2] See David Rees, *Korea: The Limited War* (1964), pt. iii, for the development of the Panmunjom armistice negotiations. During the Palais Rose Foreign Ministers Conference on Germany in early 1951, discussions on the agenda alone came to seventy-four meetings.

in Manchuria attacked UN air formations, 'some of the greatest air battles of history were fought at this time', according to the USAF Korean War historian, Robert Futrell — evidence of the achievements of Soviet technology which had also developed the hydrogen bomb during the war.

The armistice agreement, signed at Panmunjom on 27 July 1953, after Dulles had threatened Peking through Indian diplomatic channels that atomic war might soon be carried to mainland China, confirmed the partition of Korea based essentially on the battlefront of July 1951. Communist China had fought the United States to a standstill. As far as the United Nations and the United States were concerned, aggression had been repelled and collective security upheld though at the sacrifice of 140,000 US casualities. The total casualties of this great war without victory totalled four millions. Fittingly enough, Stalin's war was not ended until after Stalin's death. But by the time of the Panmunjom armistice new leaders were implementing new strategies on both sides of the iron curtain.

NEGOTIATION FROM STRENGTH?

From the very beginning of the Korean conflict the Truman administration had realised that a limited war strategy in the Far East was the only alternative to a third world war. As General Marshall, recalled as Defence Secretary during 1950–1, told the Senate Committees investigating the Far Eastern situation and MacArthur's dismissal, American policy was 'to contain Communist aggression in different fashions in different areas without resorting to total war. . . .' The United States had not extended the Korean war into the 'privileged sanctuary' of Manchuria; but neither had the Communists bombed Japan or attacked US ships supplying US forces in Korea. But the decision to limit the fighting was only one of the two major American policy decisions arising out of Korea. The other was to embark on a major rearmament programme, a programme followed in one way or another by all the NATO countries.

An American historian Marshall Shulman, has described precisely the staggering extent of the US rearmament effort during 1950–1, which went into top gear following the Chinese victories in North Korea during November–December 1950:

In January 1951 the President's State of the Union message called for an expansion of the American Air Force to 95 groups, approximately double the pre-Korean strength, with far more formidable equipment. Soviet industrial sites would be within range of the projected aircraft, even from bases in North America. In the meantime, arrangements were made to strengthen the overseas-base structure, which would immediately extend the reach of American airpower. In February it was announced that five airfields in Morocco were to be built for the United States Air Force, in addition to the large bases being developed at Wheelus Field in Libya and Dhahran in Saudi Arabia. American air units in Austria and Germany were being reinforced and reorganised as the Twelfth Air Force, a tactical unit with headquarters at Wiesbaden. In Britain, an American strategic bombing force was being further strengthened and reconstituted as the Third Air Force. . . .

Military-aircraft production capacity was to be increased to 50,000 units annually; tanks to 35,000. The armed forces were being increased to 3·5 million from 1·5 million at the outbreak of the Korean War. Defence expenditures were being projected at a rate of more than $60 billion for the next fiscal year, as contrasted with $12 billion two years before. Military and economic foreign aid was called for a level of $10·6 billion for the following fiscal year, and an increasing share of this was to be directed toward military purposes. . . . The possibility that the Korean War might develop into an all-out war with the Soviet Union had increasingly stimulated support for the intensive concentration of resources upon the hydrogen-bomb programme, as well as for an expansion of the production of atomic weapons. . . .

With four additional American divisions scheduled to be

added in 1951 to the two already stationed in Europe, the
United States was unmistakeably committed to the defence
of Europe . . . by April (1951) the Supreme Headquarters
of the Allied Powers in Europe (SHAPE) had been activated.
The same month saw the signing of the treaty for the establishment of the Coal and Steel Community among six
European nations, including the Federal Republic of
Germany. In May the United States proposed the formal
addition of Greece and Turkey to Nato; in April it was
announced that Yugoslavia, in addition to the economic
assistance it had been receiving, was now seeking military
assistance from the West. . . .[1]

This vast rearmament effort, only made politically
possible by the war in Korea, illustrated the previous
difficulties of mobilising Western public opinion to the
Communist threat in the absence of direct military
aggression. Such difficulties were shown with the resignations of Aneurin Bevan and Harold Wilson from the British
cabinet in April 1951 over the large rearmament programme
announced by the Attlee government the previous January,
resignations which contributed decisively to the collapse of
the Labour government and the Conservative victory in
October the same year. But the impetus given to Western
rearmament by Korea was immense, and in fact the force
levels of that rearmament programme have been broadly
maintained ever since. The appointment of General
Eisenhower as NATO Supreme Commander in December
1950 and the subsequent creation of a Supreme Headquarters Allied Powers, Europe (SHAPE) further underlined the fact that it had taken the Korean War to bring
about Western rearmament for all that it had been implicit
in the containment policy from the beginning.

Yet the necessity for this rearmament had been seen by
the American government ever since the news of the Soviet
atomic weapon in September 1949. The Russian bomb
showed that the policy of relying on the American atomic

[1] Marshall D. Shulman, *Stalin's Foreign Policy Reappraised* (1963),
pp. 172–3.

monopoly to deter attack might soon be obsolete. In the
next few months two immensely important decisions were
taken in Washington. In the first place, after a great secret
debate, which racked the entire US defence establishment
and was later revealed to the world during the Oppenheimer security hearings of 1954, it was decided to launch
a crash programme to make the thermonuclear bomb, 'the
so-called hydrogen or super-bomb', as Truman referred to
it when announcing the decision on 31 January 1950. At
the same time, during these early months of 1950, a
National Security Council paper, NSC-68, proposed an
American rearmament drive based on conventional as well
as nuclear forces. Politically impossible at the time when it
was drawn up, NSC-68 was partly implemented as a result
of the Korean War.

New weapons and new wars meant new attitudes. With
the evolution of NSC-68, Acheson had begun publicly to
advocate a policy of 'negotiation from strength' with the
Communist bloc. As this aspiration has continued to form
the basis of Western foreign policy ever since Acheson's first
remarks to a press conference on 8 February 1950, his words
may be quoted at length:

What we have observed over the last few years is that the
Soviet government is highly realistic and we have seen time
after time that it can adjust itself to facts when facts exist.
We have also seen that agreements reached with the Soviet
government are useful when these agreements recognise
facts or a situation which exists, and that they are not useful
when they are merely agreements which do not register
existing facts. . . . So it has been our basic policy to build
situations which will extend the area of possible agreement;
that is to create strength instead of weakness which exists in
many quarters [Acheson mentioned the recovery of West
Germany, and the Marshall Plan as examples of building
strength]. . . . These are ways in which in various parts of
the world we are trying to extend the area of possible agreement with the Soviet Union by creating situations so strong

they can be recognised, and out of them can grow agreement. . . . I don't need to go over with you again the fact
that, growing out of the last war, and other conditions before
the war and between the wars, there have been created all
over the world those positions of weakness. Every time one
of those situations exists, and they exist in Asia and they
exist in Europe, it is not only an invitation but an irresistible
invitation to the Soviet government to fish in these troubled
waters. To ask them not to fish, and to say we will have an
agreement that you won't fish is like trying to deal with a
force of nature. You can't argue with a river, it is going to
flow. You can dam it up, you can put it to useful purposes,
you can deflect it, but you can't argue with it. Therefore we
go to work . . . to change those situations of weakness so that
they won't create opportunities for fishing and opportunities
for trouble. . . .[1]

Acheson went on to sum up during the MacArthur
hearings in June 1951:

'what we must do is to create situations of strength . . . with
that change there comes a difference in the negotiating
position of the various parties, and out of that I should hope
that there would be a willingness on the side of the Kremlin
to recognise the facts . . .'.[2]

Here was a revision of the containment policy; rigid
defence of the *status quo* with its hope of Soviet 'mellowing'
was replaced by the revisionist objectives of negotiating
from increased military and political strength; diplomatic
adjustment, leading to Soviet abandonment of post-war
conquests, should be the objective of Western policy.

But the period of Acheson-inspired conventional rearmament from 1950 to 1953 also involved building political
alliances. Not only was a Japanese peace treaty signed in
September 1951, a treaty from which the Soviet Union was
excluded, and Greece and Turkey admitted to NATO in
1952, but even more important, German rearmament in a

---

[1] See the *State Department Bulletin* 20 February 1950 for Acheson's
remarks on this occasion.
[2] Senate *MacArthur Hearings*, p. 2083.

North Atlantic context was embarked on. A West German Federal Republic had been set up in 1949, without sovereignty, but — unlike the Soviet zone 'German Democratic Republic', set up the same year — based on free elections. As MacArthur's troops landed at Inchon in September 1950, the Western Foreign Ministers decided on German participation in a European defence force, a proposal approved by the NATO Lisbon meeting of February 1952, which set ambitious new goals for North Atlantic rearmament. Soon, in May 1952, with the signing of the Bonn Conventions, West Germany was given sovereignty, except for certain rights reserved to the Allies over German reunification and the Berlin question. The Conventions were to come into force with the full ratification of the European Defence Community treaty (EDC), to which, of course, the new German state was an adherent, along with the other West European countries, apart from Britain. In effect, by a triumph of diplomacy, only seven years after the end of the war, West Germany had been virtually incorporated into the Western community. That Moscow was willing in March 1952 to negotiate on a neutralised Germany was proof of a stronger Western negotiating position.

But in the event, not only was EDC (European Defence Community) doomed, but also Acheson's policy of negotiating from the strength of conventional as well as nuclear capability proved unacceptable also; it was not realised until the Kennedy era, a decade later. As the US presidential election campaign got under way in 1952 it soon became obvious that many Americans, who understandably saw the Korean War as the final perfidy of the Communist bloc, repudiated the containment policy as defeatist; and the dissatisfaction with the Democrats after twenty years of power was also exacerbated by Senator Joe McCarthy's anti-Communist campaign, which exploited the undeniable penetration of US government agencies by the Communist underground during the Roosevelt régime. (To a British observer it seems amazing that Truman and Acheson, perhaps the two most effective leaders the West has produced in the cold war, could be somehow suspected of being 'soft on Communism'.) Republican exploitation of these feelings helped to elect Eisenhower in November 1952 with a large majority. It was time for a change, and it became all the more so when less than two months after Eisenhower took office in January 1953, death came to 'the great leader of progressive mankind, J. V. Stalin', on 5 March 1953.

Even before Eisenhower's accession and Stalin's death, events were pointing towards the pattern of the next cycle of the cold war, between 1953 and 1957. In November 1952 a US thermonuclear device, made possible by a 'brilliant invention'[1] of Edward Teller's, blasted an atoll out of the Pacific at Eniwetok; an event which only preceded by nine months a similar Soviet test. Moreover, there was increasing realisation in the Soviet leadership, evidenced ever since the beginning of the Korean armistice negotiations in July 1951, that Stalin's foreign policy had almost brought the world to the verge of general war. In the Far East the Chinese Communist line had already changed by 1952 to one of tacit collaboration with 'bourgeois nationalists', for Nehru had shown over the Korean War that he was independent of Western policy; and in the Communist Party of the Soviet Union (CPSU) Nineteenth Congress in October of that year Stalin himself stressed that the imperialists were more likely to fight each other than the 'camp of socialism'. This was a breach in the Leninist doctrine of the inevitability of war between the two camps. Stalin also insisted that the 'fight for peace' — as exemplified in the Communist 'peace' campaign begun in 1949 — could develop into 'the fight for Socialism'. Political alliances with the bourgeois over the 'peace' issue were more important than social

[1] L. L. Strauss, *Men and Decisions* (1962), p. 230, Admiral Strauss is a former chairman of the AEC (Atomic Energy Commission).

change under the rigid leadership of the Party. Here was a doctrinal innovation that would be developed much further by Stalin's successors.

Indeed, by 1951-2 it was obvious that on the world stage the USSR had reached an impasse; it was diplomatically isolated, and Stalin's tactics had failed, away from areas controlled by the Red Army. China was Communist, and Moscow ruled Eastern Europe, but Greece, Persia, Turkey, Yugoslavia, South Korea and West Berlin were still outside Soviet control; France and Italy were in NATO. And in the rapidly expanding 'third world' of the former colonial lands, Stalin had alienated the 'nationalist' leaders. American leadership had created an effective armed alliance to oppose the Soviet offensive; and in halting totalitarian expansion without general war Truman and Acheson had succeeded where the men of the 1930s had failed. In the next decade, the contestants would have to manoeuvre between the new challenge of the third world and the very real possibility of a thermonuclear Armageddon.

3 1953–1957
New Men, New
Strategies

DUEL AT THE BRINK

WITH Stalin's death, G. M. Malenkov assumed the rank both of Soviet premier and of First Secretary of the CPSU (Communist Party of the Soviet Union), but within a week N. S. Khrushchev had taken over the Party secretaryship. The great succession struggle would last over four years, before Khrushchev established an undivided ascendancy over all his rivals,[1] but the first move by the oligarchy, including Molotov, Bulganin and Kaganovich, which succeeded Stalin, was to ensure its own physical survival. In June 1953 Beria, the head of the State Security Service, was arrested and executed later in the year as a criminal conspirator and agent of British intelligence. Thus began the operation of bringing the vast State Security apparatus, which had upheld Stalin's tyranny by terror, under Party control, although of course the nature of the Soviet state remained totalitarian. While consolidating its internal position, the new régime pursued a conciliatory foreign policy; the Korean armistice was signed in July, and in August Malenkov made favourable references to the Afro-Asian states, while announcing that Russia now possessed the hydrogen bomb, a claim soon confirmed by Western monitoring devices on 12 August. The virtual ending of Western nuclear ascendancy made it imperative that some attempt be made to come to a settlement of outstanding problems between the two blocs. Already in May 1953

[1] See R. Conquest, *Power and Policy in the U.S.S.R.* (1961), for an account of the Stalin succession problem and Khrushchev's rise to power.

Winston Churchill, following a course of action suggested by him first of all in 1950, had advocated a Summit meeting; and throughout late 1953 events moved towards a Foreign Ministers' meeting arranged in Berlin for January 1954.

With the Malenkov régime preoccupied with consolidating itself internally, it was left in 1953 for the New American administration to make its mark on East–West relations. And indeed, the personality of the new Secretary of State, John Foster Dulles, was to dominate not only American foreign policy, but the whole of Western strategy for the rest of the decade, until his death in 1959. Dulles had long been interested in foreign affairs, and both his grandfather and uncle had been Secretaries of State. Throughout his active political career this courageous, brilliant, subtle and sometimes infuriating man was convinced that, in all international relations, 'dynamic' spiritual values prevailed over 'static' forces, a projection of his beliefs as a practising Christian. As Dulles remarked in a much-quoted speech in December 1952 which represents his attitude during his stewardship of American foreign policy,

No iron curtain of the despots, no cringing policies of the fearful can prevent moral and spiritual forces from penetrating into the minds and souls of those under the ruthless control of the Soviet Communist structure. They will inevitably subject that structure to new thoughts, new hopes, new purposes, new standards which are bound to change the mood of the captivated and diminish the imperialist capabilities of the Soviet Communist dictators. . . .

Indeed, while actually serving as an ambassador for the Truman–Acheson régime (he was instrumental in negotiating the Japanese peace treaty), Dulles had come to feel, from both a personal and party viewpoint, that containment was a 'cringing policy of the fearful'. In a famous *Life* article in May 1952,[1] he indicated his belief that un-

[1] *A Policy of Boldness*, 19 May 1952.

c

relenting American political, economic and psychological pressure could peacefully free the Soviet satellites — thus promulgating a 'liberation' policy as an alternative to containment. During the 1952 campaign, even the more cautious Eisenhower remarked that a true peace programme would include as one of its aims 'the restoration of the captive nations'. In Dulles's words, the liberation policy would 'roll back the enemy', a phrase that the new Secretary of State often embellished with sonorous moralisms. Like Acheson, Dulles had been one of the most highly paid lawyers in the country. But unlike Acheson, who with his regard for alliances and the practical application of power, appeared as the Talleyrand of the West, Dulles projected himself as Wilsonian prosecutor of the Communist bloc for crimes against peace and liberty in the court of world opinion.

Inevitably, the events of internal and external politics soon punctured Dulles's rhetoric. A new Congress, dominated by right-wing Republicans, morbidly suspicious of 'Summit' diplomacy, was in power during the first two years of his Secretaryship; and, moreover, when his policy became much less rigid after 1955, he was checkmated by Soviet missile achievements. But already in 1953, the uncontested Soviet suppression of the East German revolt against their rule had shown that liberation, with its optimistic expectation of Soviet internal disintegration, had always been a mirage. As a consequence, Dulles's policy became characterised by the two phrases 'Massive Retaliation' and 'Brinkmanship' rather than by 'liberation' and 'roll-back'. The first of these concepts dated back to the campaign of 1952, when the Republicans wished to combine a policy of liberation with tax cuts. These two aspirations were fused, after the Eisenhower régime had taken a 'new look' at the defence budget, in Dulles's speech on 12 January 1954, in which he announced that, as the defence burden of guarding the free-world perimeter was so great, in future US strategy would 'depend primarily upon a great capacity to retaliate, instantly, by means and places of our own choosing'.

In effect, the doctrine of Massive Retaliation was a return to the pre-Korean defence strategy of the Truman administration which relied solely on the atomic deterrent; the question as to whether this was a practical policy when it came to disputes over fringe areas was answered in a long Dulles interview in *Life*[1] magazine during January 1956. Citing the US threat of atomic warfare against Peking which, Dulles stated, had been used to end the Korean War in July 1953, to underwrite the partition of Indo-China agreed upon at the 1954 Geneva Conference, and to prevent a Chinese Communist invasion of the offshore islands of Quemoy–Matsu in the winter of 1954–5, Dulles said that 'the ability to get to the verge without getting into the war is the necessary art. If you cannot master it, you inevitably get into war. If you try to run away from it, if you are scared to go to the brink, you are lost.' As Dulles rightly saw, the entire cold war was a duel at the brink.

However, in these three crises — and again in the second Quemoy episode of 1958 — Dulles manœuvred with great skill, making it quite clear to the Communists that there was a minimum position he would defend, such as Formosa, but at the same time maintaining some ambiguity as to whether he would actually fight, in defence, say, of the offshore islands. In other areas, as we shall see, Dulles set up security pacts such as SEATO and CENTO to draw the line unmistakably. But whether he talked of Brinkmanship, Massive Retaliation, or security pacts, what Dulles necessarily practised was containment, without the later Truman emphasis on conventional forces. The nuclear facts of the new cold-war balance were inescapable, and Dulles well knew it. As Emmet John Hughes, a former aide, records of Eisenhower in his splendid memoir, *The Ordeal of Power*:

[1] James Shepley, *How Dulles Averted War*, 16 January 1956.

'. . . sometimes Foster is just too worried about being accused of sounding like Truman and Acheson. I think he worries too much about it. . . .'[1]

'THE SPIRIT OF GENEVA'

Events between 1953 and 1955 soon showed how chimerical were the hopes raised in the presidental campaign of 1952 that the Eisenhower régime could negotiate with the Russians on Western terms. But Eisenhower's popularity (and prestige as a general) at least gave US policy rather more flexibility than during the last Truman–Acheson years, when negotiations with the Russians was equated with treason by many Republicans. At the same time, the much-publicised explosion of an American multi-megaton, fission-fusion-fission thermonuclear shot at Bikini in March 1954 showed the apocalyptic nature of the holocaust which could result if the cold war turned into a hot war. The US nuclear monopoly had yielded to a balance of terror. But three important international conferences during 1954–5 did in fact result in a slight relaxation of tension even if the arms race between the two super-powers still went on. In the Berlin Foreign Ministers' conference of January 1954, Molotov opposed the Western demand for free German elections, which of course would sweep away the German Democratic Republic (GDR), with a suggestion that an all-German government be formed first out of the existing régimes of West and East Germany. In effect here was the tentative beginning of the Soviet 'two Germanies' policy. Early in 1952 the Russians had been toying with the idea of a 'neutralised' Germany. Two years later, with the Soviet nuclear arsenal greatly increased, it was less of a priority for Soviet policy to exclude West Germany from the Western alliance and much more realistic to attempt to gain Western recognition of the East German régime.

[1] p. 112.

The Berlin meeting led to the Geneva Conference to discuss Korea and Indo-China, which convened in April 1954 and was attended also by the Chinese Communists. On the question of Korea the conference was unable to come to any agreement and confirmed the armistice agreement which has lasted to the present day. The decisions on Indo-China were much more important. Eisenhower's chapter on this conference in his *Memoirs* is aptly entitled 'Chaos in Indo-China',[1] and when the Foreign Ministers met in the Palais des Nations, the long, eight-year-old war in the country was about to end with the catastrophic French defeat at Dien Bien Phu. Eisenhower is rightly scathing about the French politico-military decisions which led to the fall of Dien Bien Phu in May 1954 to the Vietminh Communist insurgents. The defeat made it inevitable that the country would be partitioned and in July the Geneva conference, representing Cambodia, Laos, Vietnam and the Vietminh Communist 'Democratic Republic of Vietnam' as well as the five big powers, produced a solution — for the time being — of the Indo-China problem. A Franco-Vietminh cease-fire agreement, signed on 20 July, partitioned Vietnam along the 17th Parallel, leaving the Communists in control of the northern half of the country. The next day, 21 July, a declaration by most of the participants at Geneva noted the cease-fire agreements, looked forward to all-Vietnam elections within two years, and guaranteed the full independence and integrity of the three Indo-Chinese states — treaties to this effect had at last been negotiated by France in the year leading to the conference, including an agreement made with the Bao Dai régime in Saigon in June 1954.

South Vietnam, where Premier Ngo Din Diem, a Catholic mandarin with nationalist convictions, succeeded the French-sponsored Emperor Bao Dai as head of state in October 1955, did not adhere to the Geneva declaration,

[1] *The White House Years, 1953–1956*, vol. i, *Mandate for Change* (1963), ch. 14.

and needless to say the all-Vietnam elections were never held in 1956. Neither did the US government adhere to the declaration, for Dulles wished to keep American freedom of action in the area, was wary of Congressional reaction to the agreement and was rightly sceptical of Communist intentions. Instead the US issued a separate statement to the effect that it would not use force to disturb the Geneva agreements, while looking forward to UN-supervised elections in Vietnam.

To understand Dulles's rather odd attitude to this conference (he abruptly left Geneva after the first week, handing over to Under-Secretary of State Bedell Smith) it must be recalled that, even before the conference met at Geneva, Dulles had wanted to deter Chinese Communist intervention in Indo-China with the announcement of a Western-inspired security pact, backed with force if necessary. Eden, whose personal relations with Dulles were bad, refused to support such a pact before the conference, a decision for which Dulles never forgave him. Eden has rightly been given much credit for his handling of the Geneva conference, yet, ultimately, the partition of Vietnam was enforced by the hubbub of speculation about American intentions. When Dulles publicly stated, for example, in September 1953 that Chinese intervention 'could not occur without grave consequences which might not be confined to Indo-China' he helped to ensure that the Vietminh would come no further south than the 17th Parallel immediately following their victory over the French at Dien Bien Phu.[1]

Events later in the winter of 1954–55 ended this phase of turmoil in the Far East. Following the Geneva settlement, the South-East Asia Treaty Organisation (SEATO) was

[1] Eden comments that Geneva 1954 was the first international conference at which he was 'sharply conscious of the deterrent power of the hydrogen bomb. I was grateful for it. I do not think we could have got through the Geneva conference and avoided a major war without it.' *Full Circle* (1960), p. 123.

formed in September 1954 by the United States of America, the United Kingdom, France, Thailand, Pakistan, Australia, and New Zealand, guaranteeing the area, including South Vietnam, Laos and Cambodia, against formal aggression. And in January 1955, as the Chinese Communists threatened the Nationalist-held offshore islands of Quemoy and Matsu, which were in sight of the Chinese mainland, Eisenhower obtained a Congressional Resolution empowering the executive to defend Formosa and the Pescadores; the offshore islands were not specifically mentioned in the resolution or in the US–Chinese Nationalist security pact signed a few weeks before, but there was sufficient ambiguity in American intentions to make the Chinese Communists desist. When Chou En-lai, Mao's prime minister, attended the Afro-Asian conference at Bandung in April 1955, he radiated goodwill, spoke of the 'peaceful' liberation of Taiwan, and for the next three years the Far Eastern front of the cold war was quiescent.

Meanwhile, in Europe the drift towards the Geneva Summit Conference of 1955 was under way. Both sides imagined that they were in a strong negotiating position. At the end of 1953 Dulles had been so concerned with the failure of the French chamber to ratify EDC that he had threatened an 'agonizing reappraisal' of American involvement in Europe if the master-scheme to rearm West Germany fell through. The French *did* reject the EDC treaty in August 1954, but, thanks to some inspired diplomacy on the part of both Dulles and Eden, an alternative formula was found for German participation in the Western alliance. As a result of the London Conference and the Paris Agreements of September–October 1954, West Germany was admitted into the revived Western European Union of the Brussels Pact, and to NATO;[1] on 5 May 1955 the Paris Agreements came into force and the Federal Republic formally became part of the Western Alliance.

[1] See Appendix C.

There was parallel activity in Moscow. In February 1955, Malenkov was replaced by Bulganin, but it was immediately clear that Khrushchev was the driving force of the 'collective leadership'. A defence reorganisation of the Soviet armed forces began, the East European countries set up a joint command in May known as the Warsaw Pact (an answer to the West German admission to NATO and WEU) and the first Russian intermediate-range ballistic missile (IRBM) was test-fired that spring. The Soviet leaders were letting the West know that, if necessary, they were preparing to fight a nuclear war. At the same time, as part of the emerging 'coexistence' policy, Khrushchev patched up the Soviet quarrel with Yugoslavia and agreed to an Austrian State Treaty neutralising the country in May 1955.

Much was expected in the West of the Geneva Summit Conference which met in July 1955. It was even believed that the advantage lay with the West. The exchanges between the four leaders, and especially between Eisenhower and Bulganin and Khrushchev were affable; but the USSR made it quite clear during the conference that only with the dismantling of NATO could they agree to German reunification; and failing that impossible blackmailing demand it became plain that Communism in East Germany was just not negotiable — neither was the *status quo* in Eastern Europe. Indeed, the Soviet terms for German unity — the withdrawal of US forces from Western Europe — had hardened since the Berlin Conference of January 1954, a further reflection of the changing power-balance between the two contestants in the cold war. Eisenhower's account of the Geneva Conference reflects his bitterness at the failure of the meeting:

The Summit Conference had been hailed by the world as a great success, even a diplomatic triumph for the West. It had been held in a cordial atmosphere, which represented a sharp departure from the vitriolic recriminations which have characterised so many meetings in the past. Agreements had been reached to study ways of increasing friendship between the peoples of the West and of the Soviet Union, and these contacts could, we thought, presage the beginning of a more open society in the USSR. More surprising had been the Soviet agreement (in the conference communiqué) that 'the settlement of the German question and the reunification of Germany by free elections shall be carried out in conformity with the national interests of the German people and interests of European security', an agreement which, if acted on, would have done much to re-establish stability and progress among the peoples of the European continent. Most spectacular, in the eyes of the press and the public, had been our opportunity to demonstrate to the world, in the Open Skies (armaments inspection) proposal, the dedication of the United States to world peace and disarmament and our sincerity in offering a concrete way in which we would participate.

Then disillusionment had followed. At the October Foreign Ministers' Conference, held in the same room as the Summit Conference, the Soviets had repudiated every measure to which they had agreed in July. Unfortunately, this received less attention in the press than had the earlier agreements. . . . But to those of us responsible for the conduct of foreign relations, the Soviet duplicity was a grievous disappointment indeed. In the final analysis, however, I believe the Geneva Conference represented a limited success. The record was established: all could now see the nature of Soviet diplomatic tactics as contrasted with those of the Free World. Peoples had been given a glowing picture of hope and, though it was badly blurred by the Soviets, at least the outlines of the picture remained. Moreover, and in spite of what happened thereafter, the cordial atmosphere of the talks, dubbed the 'Spirit of Geneva', never faded entirely. Indeed, the way was opened for some increase in intercourse between East and West — there began, between the United States and Russia, exchanges of trade exhibitions, scientists, musicians, and other performers; visits were made by Mikoyan and Kozlov to the United States, and returned by Vice-President Nixon and my brother, Milton, to the Soviet Union and Poland. These were small beginnings, but they could not have transpired in the atmosphere before Geneva. . . .[1]

[1] Eisenhower, *Mandate for Change*, pp. 529-30.

Of course, for the Soviets 'the increase in intercourse' between East and West agreed at Geneva was but a tactic in their 'coexistence' policy. Moreover, there was no contradiction at all in Communist thinking between the July communiqué on Germany with its promise of free elections and Molotov's specific repudiation of this apparent promise in October. The promise of 'free elections' had been qualified in Soviet eyes by the 'escape clause' that they should 'be carried out in conformity with the national interests of the German people . . . ,' for to Moscow 'the German people' were represented by the *East* German régime; i.e. by the very phraseology of the Geneva communiqué, Khrushchev and Bulganin were stating that they would not really agree to measures such as free elections which might result in the elimination of the Ulbricht satellite régime of the Soviet zone of Germany. And, indeed, even the exchanges of high-echelon politicians which so pleased Eisenhower eventually resulted in the 'vitriolic recriminations' of Nixon's 'kitchen debate' with Khrushchev in July 1959.

Thus the only Summit of the 1950s ended merely with an agreement on cultural exchanges, and a fruitless attempt by the Soviet to capitalise on the 'Spirit of Geneva' for possible Western concessions, including the dismantling of NATO. And as no concessions were forthcoming, the essential dynamics of the cold war remained unaltered, though with the Soviet position, if anything, strengthened.

THE STRATEGY OF COEXISTENCE

No sooner was the Geneva Summit Conference over, with its tacit acceptance of the *status quo* in Europe by both sides, than the Middle East became a theatre of the cold war.[1] Within just over a year of Geneva the area was in flames

[1] See in this series, Ann Williams, *Britain and France in the Middle East. 1914 to the aftermath of Suez.*

with the Suez war; the Russians threatened London and
Paris with rocket attacks, and, preserving the amenities, the
United States let it be publicly known that in the event of
such attacks, ' the Soviet Union would be destroyed'.

The roots of this great crisis go back to 1953, when Dulles
became interested in organising a security pact among the
nations on the southern border of the USSR, the so-called
'Northern Tier' of the Middle Eastern countries. Eventually
the pact was completed at Baghdad in April 1955, Turkey,
Iraq and Britain being signatories. Pakistan and Persia
joined the Baghdad Pact a few months later. Valuable as the
pact was in the event of Soviet aggression, it had disturbed
the fragile equilibrium of the Middle East; Colonel Nasser's
Egypt saw in Iraq a rival for the leadership of the Arab
world and retaliated by stepping up the pressure against
Israel with guerrilla attacks and by asking the Western
powers for more arms. No military aid was forthcoming
from the West, so the Russians, already interested in the
area and suspicious of the Baghdad Pact, were only too
ready to supply tanks, arms, and aircraft, including MIG
fighters and jet bombers, to Egypt. The Egyptian arms
deal, siphoned through Czechoslovakia, was announced in
September.

At the same time Nasser was hoping to build the Aswan
High Dam with Anglo-American aid, helped by the World
Bank. By the spring of 1956, Nasser had recognised Communist China, another (Chinese) arms deal was rumoured,
and, inevitably but abruptly, offers of Anglo-American aid
for the Aswan Dam were revoked by Dulles and the British
in July. It is a moot point whether Nasser had already
planned the nationalisation of the Suez Canal when he
decided to play off the United States against the USSR.
Dulles, however, suspicious of neutralism at this time, had
no hesitation in letting the world know that the United
States could not be blackmailed in this manner. Unfortunately for the Western alliance, Nasser almost immediately

nationalised the Suez Canal on 26 July 1956. Three months later, after the signing of a written agreement at Sèvres on 23 October, Britain, France and Israel attacked Egypt,[1] only to be halted by pressure applied by the United States and the UN. With all the various strands that made up the November 1956 crisis, we are not concerned here. But two general considerations must be mentioned, as relevant to the cold war, rather than to the Middle East power-balance. In the first place, why did Anglo-American policy diverge so much? — for here was the most serious rupture between the two countries during the entire period of the cold war. Secondly, how far was the Suez intervention related to the Hungarian uprising? — an insurrection which was crushed by Soviet troops in the same month as Suez, a repression often described as having been made possible by the attack on Port Said and the Canal.

Firstly, a possible cause for Anglo-American differences over Suez may be looked for less in formal, political differences, which occur inevitably between the closest allies, than in the appalling personal relationship of Eden and Dulles.[2] Both Eisenhower and Dulles were firmly convinced that the use of force against Egypt over the Canal was not morally justified, that it would increase the distrust of the West among the Afro-Asian neutrals, and that, in any case, American support for it would be unwise, since there was a US presidential election pending. Also, Eisenhower had listened to British reservations over Indo-China in April 1954; it was intolerable to Washington that

[1] See Herman Finer, *Dulles Over Suez* (1964), ch. 13, and, more particularly, Terence Robertson, *Crisis: The Inside Story of the Suez Conspiracy* (1965), for the details of Anglo-French-Israeli co-ordination. Both writers draw extensively on French and Israeli sources, including the apparently reliable evidence of the French foreign minister in 1956, M. Pineau, and high Israeli officials, who were directly concerned with the Sèvres understanding.

[2] See R. Goold-Adams, *The Time of Power: A Re-appraisal of John Foster Dulles* (1962), for a detailed and convincing account of the relationship between Eden and Dulles.

the British should 'go it alone' over Suez. Yet even when one recognises these factors, the extreme distrust and dislike between the emotional Eden and the legalistic Dulles, which all commentators and historians record, was surely the crucial factor leading to Suez. Dulles's pedantic approach almost certainly drove Eden, already in ill-health, into the use of force with his French allies, out of distrust of Dulles's good faith. With any other combination of Secretary of State and Prime Minister since 1945 the tragedy could probably have been avoided. In 1956 it was unavoidable.

In the second place, the crisis of November 1956 in Budapest arose from Khrushchev's fundamental recasting of Soviet strategy in the CPSU (Communist Party of the Soviet Union) Twentieth Congress in February 1956. Khrushchev's speeches in this historic Congress may be considered under two headings, internal and external. As far as Communist global policy was concerned Khrushchev ended the Cominform 'two camps' policy of 1947, and outlined the new strategy of 'peaceful coexistence':

1. Peaceful coexistence was not a tactical expedient (as under Malenkov) but a fundamental of Communist foreign policy, based on the 'certainty' of Communist victory. There was no third way between war and peaceful coexistence.

2. Khrushchev modified Marxist–Leninist orthodoxy to say that war was not, in his own words, 'a fatalistic inevitability'. The 'mighty social and political forces' of the socialist world could stop the imperialists from launching war.

3. There was an increasing possibility of non-violent transformation to socialism. Socialism without revolution might be an important way towards Communism.

In effect, the Soviet leaders had recognised that a new dogma was necessary in the thermonuclear age; peaceful coexistence was a formula which was supposed to bring about the victory of Communism without the risks of nuclear war.[1] In particular, as we shall see, when backed with Soviet technical, military, and economic advances, the new doctrine of the economic superiority of Communism would have special relevance to the problem of East–West rivalry in the under-developed countries.

As far as the internal policy of the party was concerned, Khrushchev, in his famous 'secret speech' of 25 February 1956, denounced Stalin as a megalomaniac tyrant, a paranoiac murderer who liquidated the best cadres of the Party in the Great Purges, set up labour camps, deported entire Soviet nationalities, wrecked Russian strategy at the opening of the Second World War, framed the famous Jewish doctors, and perverted 'socialist legality' into a monstrous personality cult. Khrushchev's denunciation of Stalin has been invoked so often that parts of it should be quoted here:

After Stalin's death the Central Committee of the party began to implement a policy of explaining concisely and consistently that it is impermissible and foreign to the spirit of Marxism–Leninism to elevate one person, to transform him into a superman possessing supernatural characteristics akin to those of a god. Such a man supposedly knows everything, sees everything, thinks for everyone, can do anything, is infallible in his behaviour. Such a belief about a man, and specifically about Stalin, was cultivated among us for many years. . . . At the present we are concerned with a question which has immense importance for the party now and for the future . . . with how the cult of the person of Stalin has been gradually growing, the cult which became at a certain specific stage the source of a whole series of

[1] 'Peaceful coexistence is a specific form of class struggle between socialism and capitalism. The socialist system is victorious in worldwide competition with capitalism, because the socialist mode of production has a decisive advantage over the capitalist mode of production. There is no contradiction whatsoever between the Marxist–Leninist position concerning the inevitability of the victory of Communism and peaceful coexistence. . . .'

Quoted from the official Diplomatic Dictionary edited by Foreign Minister Gromyko (Moscow, 1960) in C. Black and T. Thornton (ed.), *Communism and Revolution* (1964), p. 433.

exceedingly serious and grave perversions of party principles, of party democracy, of revolutionary legality. . . .
During Lenin's life the Central Committee of the party was
a real expression of collective leadership of the party, and
of the nation. Being a militant Marxist–revolutionist, always
unyielding in matters of principle, Lenin never imposed by
force his views upon his co-workers. He tried to convince
some; he patiently explained his opinions to others . . .
[and] his acute mind . . . detected in Stalin . . . those
negative characteristics which resulted later in grave consequences. Fearing the future fate of the party and of the
Soviet nation, pointing out that it was necessary to consider
the question of transferring Stalin from the position of
Secretary-General because of the fact that Stalin is ex-
cessively rude, that he does not have a proper attitude towards his comrades, that he is capricious and abuses his
power. In December 1922 . . . [Lenin] wrote:

> After taking over the position of Secretary General,
> Comrade Stalin accumulated in his hands immeasurable
> power and I am not certain whether he will be always
> able to use this power with the required care.

. . . The negative characteristics of Stalin, which, in Lenin's
time, were only incipient, transformed themselves during
the last years into a grave abuse of power by Stalin, which
caused untold harm to our party . . . Stalin acted not
through persuasion, . . . but by imposing his concepts and
demanding absolute submission to his opinion. Whoever
opposed this concept . . . was doomed to subsequent moral
and physical annihilation . . . Stalin originated the concept
'enemy of the people'. This term automatically rendered it
unnecessary that the ideological errors of a man or men
engaged in a controversy be proven; this term made
possible the usage of the most cruel repression, violating all
norms of revolutionary legality, against anyone who in any
way disagreed with Stalin . . . [a term] introduced for the
purpose of physically annihilating such individuals. . . .

Khrushchev went on to give a selective account of the
history of the Great Purges:

. . . Stalin's wilfulness vis-à-vis the party and its Central
Committee became fully evident after the seventeenth

party congress, which took place in 1934 . . . of the 139
members and candidates of the party's Central Committee
who were elected at the seventeenth congress . . . 70% were
arrested and shot (*Indignation in the hall*). . . . Mass repression
grew tremendously from the end of 1936. . . . Stalin put the
Party and the NKVD up to the use of mass terror when the
exploiting classes had been liquidated. . . . the terror was
actually directed not at the remnants of the defeated
exploiting classes but against the honest workers of the party
and of the Soviet State. . . . confessions of guilt of many
arrested and charged with enemy activity were gained with
the help of cruel and inhuman tortures. . . . NKVD workers
manufactured various fictitious 'anti-Soviet centres'. . . .
many thousands of honest and innocent Communists have
died as a result of this monstrous falsification of such
'cases'. . . . Stalin had sanctioned . . . the most brutal
violation of Socialist legality, torture and oppression. . . .

But as Khrushchev made clear, Stalin's crimes were not
only against the party, for his mania had also 'led to serious
consequences during the great patriotic war'. All warnings
from Churchill about the coming German attack had been
ignored, and there were as well serious results on army
morale of 'large-scale repressions against the military
cadres' during the Purges:

Therefore, the threatening danger which hung over our
fatherland in the first period of the war was largely due to
the faulty methods of directing the nation and party by
Stalin himself . . . the nervousness and hysteria which Stalin
demonstrated, interfering with actual military operations,
caused our army serious damage . . . [yet] in various ways
he tried to inculcate in the people the version that all
victories gained by the Soviet nation during the great
patriotic war were due to the courage, daring and genius
of Stalin and no one else . . . crude violations of the basic
Leninist principles of the nationality policy of the Soviet
state. We refer to the mass deportations from their native
places of whole nations, together with all Communists and
Komsomols without any exception; this deportation action
was not dictated by any military considerations. . . . the
Ukrainians avoided meeting this fate only because there

were too many of them and there was no place to which to
deport them. . . .

After the war the situation went from bad to worse:

> . . . after the war the situation became even more com-
> plicated. Stalin became even more capricious, irritable and
> brutal; in particular his suspicion grew. His persecution
> mania reached unbelievable dimensions . . . cleverly taken
> advantage of by the abject provocateur and vile enemy,
> Beria, who murdered thousands of Communists and loyal
> Soviet people. . . . conflict with Yugoslavia. . . . Stalin's
> mania for greatness. . . . suspicion and haughtiness not in
> relation to individuals in the USSR but in relation to whole
> parties and nations. . . . 'The affair of the doctor-plotters'
> (*Animation in the hall*). Actually there was no 'affair'.
> . . . Academician Vinogradov put in chains. . . . Stalin
> personally called the investigating judge, gave him in-
> structions . . . beat, beat, and once again beat . . . shameful
> facts. . . . absurd and ridiculous suspicion that Voroshilov
> was an English agent (*Laughter in the hall*). It's true — an
> English agent! . . .[1]

With this Grand Guignol production of much of the
Soviet Union's history, Khrushchev, who tactfully omitted to
remind his audience that Beria had been liquidated only
two years previously, on charges of being an agent of British
intelligence, and that he himself had been a leading Stalinist
until 5 March 1953, was of course not only making a play
for the supreme leadership of the party and state by labelling
his opponents as Stalinists. In stating that the Stalin terror
was over he was also dovetailing his external and internal
policies. He was presenting the Soviet Union as an advanced
modern state, worthy in every respect to challenge the US
for world leadership — a programme with particular appeal
to the newly-emerging class of Soviet technologists.

Yet the first results of the Twentieth Congress were felt in

---

[1] See *The Dethronement of Stalin* (1956) for the full text of the secret
speech; the transcript was leaked to the State Department from a Communist source believed to be Polish.

the Eastern bloc, rather than in the West. In Poland riots against the Stalinist régime broke out in June, and in October the revisionist Communist Gomulka was reluctantly accepted as prime minister by Moscow as the only alternative to a national uprising. In Poland, the Party remained loyal to Moscow on external policy, but in Hungary, where the entire Communist apparatus was swept away by a national revolution a few days after the change of government in Warsaw, Soviet military intervention was ordered after some debate among the Soviet leadership. On 1 November 1956 the government of Imre Nagy took Hungary out of the Warsaw Pact; four days later seven Russian divisions went into action against the Nagy régime. Limited war had been declared against the Hungarian people to bring them back into 'the camp of Socialism'.

As the *UN Report on Hungary* makes clear, the complex dispositions of the Soviet invasion, which ended with the eventual murder of Nagy, presumably on Khrushchev's orders, were not triggered by the Suez crisis. . . . 'the military reoccupation of Hungary which preceded the attack [on Budapest] and made it possible could not have owed its origin to the Middle East crisis.'[1] What Suez and Hungary did do was to obscure for a year the full significance of the emergence of the 'coexistence' policy. Events in 1957 would make it clear that the West faced a new Communist offensive more dangerous than Stalin's, in that the USSR now had missile capability to attack US cities.

SPUTNIK: 4 OCTOBER 1957

Throughout the first few months of 1957 both East and West tried frantically to mend the fences blasted down by Suez and Hungary. Eastern European leaders were summoned to Moscow, and promised economic concessions,

[1] Malcolm Mackintosh, *Strategy and Tactics of Soviet Foreign Policy* (1962), p. 178.

while to the West the Soviet Union made tentative approaches in the fields of disarmament, economic co-operation and trade. By May, Khrushchev was suggesting a new Summit meeting, in an attempt to revive the Spirit of Geneva. Then, in June 1957, Khrushchev finally eliminated the 'anti-Party group' of Malenkov, Molotov, Kaganovich and Shepilov inside the Soviet leadership.

While Khrushchev successfully manœuvred during the early months of 1957 to establish his undisputed authority inside the USSR, Western leaders were also active. In March, President Eisenhower conferred at Bermuda with Prime Minister Macmillan, who succeeded Eden in January 1957. It was agreed that Thor IRBMs (inter-mediate-range ballistic missiles) should be stationed in Britain; and in October the two leaders again met in Washington to implement nuclear co-operation between Britain and the US. Macmillan had restored, as far as it ever could be restored, the Anglo-American understanding which would now be based, of course, on Britain's irre-versibly subordinate rôle in the alliance. This reliance on the nuclear defences of the West was unmistakably emphasised when in May it was decided to arm NATO with nuclear weapons. In December, the NATO Council meeting, in Paris at Heads-of-Government level, confirmed these decisions; moreover, IRBMs were to be placed in Italy, Turkey and Greece.

But the October meeting between Eisenhower and Mac-millan and the NATO meeting of December took place after the momentous development of Soviet inter-continental ballistic missile (ICBM) capability, which entirely changed the strategic relationship between Moscow and the West. On 26 August 1957 the Soviet news agency, Tass, announced that the Soviet Union had successfully tested an ICBM (inter-continental ballistic missile) — the Russians had beaten the Americans in the race for the ultimate weapon. That the Soviet claim was indeed true was shown by the spectacular Soviet launching of the first earth satellite, Sputnik I, on 4 October; the whole world could hear — and even see — the proof of Soviet missile mastery as it orbited in space. . . . the *bleep-bleep-bleep* of Sputnik truly marked the end of the first great strategic phase of the cold war. For although the USSR had exploded atomic (1949) and thermonuclear (1953) weapons, and had developed a long-range bomber force (1954–5), until Sputnik the delivery capability of the US Strategic Air Command had still a decisive superiority. Even more important, there had been, ever since the beginning of the cold war, an unconscious assumption in the West of the superiority of its technology. That assumption could no longer be held; the whole globe now lay open to Soviet thermonuclear missiles.

We shall see how in the next few years a tremendous race took place between the United States and the USSR for strategic superiority. Within a few weeks of Sputnik a general conference of the world Communist Parties took place in Moscow, as if to put the final finishing touches to the 'peaceful coexistence' strategy. Later analysis showed that the Moscow Declaration of November 1957 by the twelve ruling Communist parties confirmed the emergence of the Sino-Soviet split, which many date as beginning with the CPSU Twentieth Congress. But at the time it seemed as if the Communist bloc was more confident than ever before of final victory.

The Moscow Declaration laid down the ends and means of the revolution in a world-wide 'dictatorship of the proletariat' which would bring about universal socialism and later Communism. Stalin had attempted to expand the Communist empire by direct use of armed force; inevitably he had been halted by a coalition of his enemies who threatened war if he advanced further. Khrushchev's policy of 1957 was even more ambitious. In a grand offensive led by the USSR, 'the third world' would be subverted; anti-colonial and colonial and nationalist sentiment on a global scale would be exploited in the fight against the West; and Soviet achievements in space and on the earth would provide a vast totalitarian public relations programme to show the neutrals that Communism was the 'wave of the future'. Most important of all, using the political and psychological threat of Soviet ICBMs, Moscow's missile diplomacy would paralyse the NATO European allies, while isolating the now-vulnerable heartland of the imperialists, the United States. The 'iron laws of historic inevitability' were bound to bring about 'bourgeois-democratic' and finally 'socialist' revolutions as part of the wave of the future. And the story of the cold war in the next five years is the story of Khrushchev's great offensive and how it was halted, with the world on the verge of nuclear war, in the Cuban missile crisis of October 1962.

4 1957–1962
The Wave of the Future

A FEW days after the orbiting of Sputnik, the mood of the
United States, as it pressed on with its own Titan and Atlas
ICBM programme, was well expressed by the *Christian
Science Monitor*: 'Military — and diplomatic — logic today
is posing one single desperately essential task for the United
States. That is to catch up, at whatever cost, with the Soviet
Union in missile development.' (Following numerous fiascos
the first American Atlas ICBM was fired from Cape
Canaveral on 17 December 1957.) As if recognising that his
grand strategy of 'Massive Retaliation' was dead, there was
an article by Dulles in the October 1957 edition of *Foreign
Affairs* which noted that 'in the future it may be feasible to
place less reliance upon deterrence of vast retaliatory
power. . . .'. The wheel had come round to the ideas of the
containment policy which had been elaborated in the same
magazine ten years before by George Kennan.

But the initiative remained with the Soviets. With
Russian diplomacy active throughout the under-developed
world, Moscow persistently tried from the end of 1957 to
force an accommodation on its own terms with the West as
part of the coexistence policy. A prime target of Soviet
propaganda was NATO's nuclear arsenal. There were
threats, offers of 'zones of peace', disarmament proposals —
the Geneva nuclear test-ban talks opened in October 1958
— and ceaseless reiteration of the menace of West German
re-armament, a leading theme of Communist propaganda.
In March 1958 the USSR announced a series of thermo-

nuclear tests; while at the same time it supported the Rapacki plan for a nuclear-free zone in central Europe; acceptance of the plan would mean, inevitably, that West Germany would be open to Soviet conventional aggression or para-military subversion.

However, it was manifest that following Sputnik there would have to be some adjustment of Europe's relation to the United States within the Nato alliance. In the first place, by the middle of the 1950s, thanks to the Marshall Plan, Western Europe had economically recovered from the war. Western European Union and the various institutions associated with the Marshall Plan had furthered the feeling of unity in the area. During 1951–52 'The Six' — Benelux, Italy, France and West Germany — had set up the European Coal and Steel Community, and after years of patient negotiation the same countries in March 1957 signed the Treaty of Rome which created the European Economic Community, to come into effect on 1 January 1958. The preamble to the treaty stated that the signatories wished to establish an ever-closer union to secure economic and social progress by common action to eliminate barriers in Europe — a dream of centuries seemed to be coming true, almost as a by-product of the cold war.

Europe's resurgence antedated Sputnik, but the military problems raised by the new Soviet missiles are still with us. Before Sputnik, America guaranteed Western Europe; after Sputnik, with American cities open to Soviet attack, America still needed Europe to maintain her balance of power. But some Europeans had lost faith in the US deterrent; would the Americans, they wondered, trade Paris for Chicago in the event of war? The attempt to achieve Allied collaboration in an effective NATO deterrent began at the time of Sputnik, and culminated five years later in the stillborn plan for a Multilateral Force (MLF); but to some Europeans, like General de Gaulle, national deterrents seemed a better bet, while to others again, such as the supporters of the British Campaign for Nuclear Disarmament, neutralism seemed the best prescription for survival.

Yet, as Khrushchev's next move at Berlin was to show, there was no serious alternative to Western unity and firmness in the face of the Soviet threat. The launching of Sputnik was followed by a Soviet diplomatic offensive, which included proposals for a new Summit Conference; these suggestions showed that in early 1958 Moscow was still confident that high level talks were a better way of forcing an Allied retreat over Nato's nuclear weapons than political and psychological threats. The drive to the Summit was halted, however, by two crises in the summer of 1958. The Iraqi government was overthrown by a nationalist rising in July, and although Moscow failed to prevent British and American precautionary military moves into Jordan and Lebanon, Iraq left the Baghdad Pact — later renamed the Central Treaty Organisation (CENTO). There were also significant developments in the Far East, when, in August, the Chinese Communists again threatened Quemoy–Matsu. It was Dulles's last great crisis, and for the second time in his secretaryship, by astute use of ambiguous threats, he forced Peking to abandon the proposed invasion of the islands.

No sooner were the guns at Quemoy silenced in October than Khrushchev moved to regain the initiative — at Berlin. His earlier moves in the spring and summer of 1958 had failed to produce the concessions which would stabilise his Western front on his own terms. Now, in November 1958, just a decade after Stalin's great challenge, the Soviet leader dramatically decided to raise the stakes for a settlement favourable to Moscow, a move that would almost inevitably produce the much-desired Summit Conference. In Moscow on 10 November Khrushchev declared that the Potsdam signatories should renounce 'the remnants of the occupation régime in Berlin', a demand followed on

27 November by Soviet proposals suggesting that Berlin should become a demilitarised free city on the territory of the GDR (German Democratic Republic), which should inherit all Soviet access rights. After six months the Soviet Union would unilaterally 'execute the measures indicated' with the GDR.

As the outcome of this scheme, if adhered to, could only have been war, Khrushchev retreated from this ultimatum. In doing so he set in motion a series of events against a backcloth of rumour, tension, fear and alarm that included Macmillan's visit to Moscow in February 1959, the death of the indomitable Dulles in May, the Geneva Foreign Ministers' Conference in the summer, Khrushchev's visit to the US in August, and the failed Paris Summit Conference of May 1960. This conference was aborted, with Khrushchev piqued, after a Soviet ground-to-air missile destroyed an American U-2 reconnaissance aircraft deployed over Sverdlovsk. But there was a significant difference of *kind* between Soviet pressure over Berlin in 1958 and on earlier occasions:

It was the first ['negotiation'] crisis in which Russian policy can be said to be that of a revisionist rather than a *status quo* power. Earlier Russian demands for negotiation, whether at the summit or elsewhere, had been based essentially on the wish to prevent something happening; to prevent the integration of West Germany into the Western camp, to prevent the EDC treaty from being ratified, to prevent the WEU from being set up, to prevent Western intervention in Iraq or Lebanon or Jordan. With the Berlin crisis of 1958-60 the demand for negotiation arises for the first time from Soviet revisionism, from the Soviet demand for change in the status of Berlin. . . .[1]

As Khrushchev told Walter Lippmann at this time, 'the revolution is the *status quo*'. Thus throughout the Berlin crisis, and indeed, until the Cuban confrontation of 1962, Khrushchev's coexistence policy was essentially a demand

[1] Coral Bell, *Negotiation From Strength* (1962), p. 177.

to the West to accede to his revisionist claims while carrying a strategy of economic penetration to the third world. And it must be admitted that Soviet policy, with the threats of its Sputnik and missile diplomacy alternating with the vistas of the economic millenium of the wave of the future presented a much more psychologically appealing vision of Communist victory than Stalin's Orwellian decrees. But apart from the faithful, not only neutralists and those generally sympathetic to Soviet aims were responding favourably to Khrushchev's campaign. It is significant that some well-known non-Communist Western politicians were also sympathetic. It appears, for example, that during 1959–60, the British Labour ideologist Richard Crossman was predicting 'with mathematical certainty' that the West was bound to be defeated in every kind of peaceful competition with the East, and was 'hotly insisting that instead of co-operating inside the capitalist system [the British] Labour [Party] should wait till capitalism crashed.'[1]

In any case, until 1960 Khrushchev seems to have assumed that it was possible to extract voluntary concessions from Eisenhower ('the Spirit of Camp David'); whilst following the presidential election of 1960 he also seems to have assumed, as we shall see, that it would be possible to force concessions from the new president by intimidation. Yet while the Berlin crisis was unfolding between 1958 and 1961 Khrushchev's entire eastern flank was rolled up by a series of events which we can now see constituted the most serious internal crisis in the whole history of the international Communist movement — the Sino-Soviet split.

THE GREAT SCHISM: MOSCOW/PEKING

While Khrushchev waited in November 1960 to confront the new American president with his demands over Berlin,

[1] See *The Observer* 'Profile' of Crossman, 28 March 1965.

the Moscow Conference of eighty-one Communist Parties convened in the Soviet capital. Its final declaration seemed as confident of victory as that of the general Communist conclave three years before:

Today it is the world socialist system and the forces fighting against imperialism for a socialist transformation of society that determine the main content, main trend, and main features of the historical development of society. Whatever efforts imperialism makes, it cannot stop the advance of history. A reliable basis has been provided for further decisive victories for socialism. The complete triumph of socialism is inevitable. . . .

The Moscow Declaration superficially reflected Soviet strategy in the struggle with the West; and it only came to be gradually understood during 1961, that the Moscow Conference 'was probably the most important gathering of its kind in the entire history of Communism . . . it ended one phase of Communist history and began another which will have a lasting impact on Soviet policy, Sino-Soviet relations, and the future evolution of relations within the Communist movement. . . .'[1] Ever since 1956 there had been growing and decisive differences between Moscow and Peking over a whole range of questions involving Communist theory, strategy and tactics both in intra-bloc relations and over the cold war with the West. The price of the ostensible Soviety victory on the drafting of the 1960 Moscow Declaration was the recognition throughout the entire Communist movement, a recognition that was soon to percolate through to the West, that Moscow's writ no longer ran on a world-wide basis and that a Sino-Soviet schism had become a reality. No one can tell where this schism will end.

Of course there has always been significant differences between the Soviet and Chinese parties. As we have seen,

[1] Donald S. Zagoria, *The Sino-Soviet Conflict 1956–61* (1965), pp. 343, 366.

Mao's peasant-based guerrilla armies had achieved victory with minimal Soviet advice and assistance. In Sinifying Leninism, Mao has always regarded himself as a creative interpreter of Communist doctrine, on the level of Marx and Lenin. At best, Khrushchev was no more than a pragmatic Russian politician. Then again, there is a strong nationalist component in Maoism, indeed in many ways Mao Tse-tung is a direct descendant of the great emperors of the Middle Kingdom. And not only had the interests of the revolution in China been subordinated to Soviet state interests in the 1920s and 1940s, but pre-1917 Russia had always had a bad imperialist record in its dealings with China.

As we now know, all these factors have helped to bring about the Sino-Soviet split. But there is a great deal of evidence to show that it was not until 1956 that Peking freed itself from its dependence on the CPSU, and seriously began to differ with Moscow. The CCP disagreed with Khrushchev's de-Stalinisation campaign — the dead dictator's virtues exceeded his faults in the Chinese view — and tended also to dissent from the views that Khrushchev still held on the necessary subordination of other Communist parties to Moscow. In fact, the Chinese tended to agree with the Italian Communist leader Togliatti, who in a famous post-Twentieth Congress article advocated a new 'polycentric' Communist movement of equal parties. When Poland and Hungary rebelled at the end of 1956 the Chinese were not slow to criticise Moscow. The foundations for the later schism were already laid, for Moscow's apparently infallible authority had been irretrievably weakened.

Then, in 1957, came Sputnik. Latent contradictions of personality and nationality there may have been, but fundamentally the Sino-Soviet split had been conducted in terms of Communist theory. 'Without a revolutionary theory, there can be no revolutionary movement', is a statement repeated scores of times by Lenin, for if strategy is the link between the theory and day-to-day tactics, then theory is the Marxist–Leninist expression of historical reality. And in 1957, as a result of Soviet missile triumphs, the Chinese interpreted 'reality' as indicating, in Mao's words, 'the East wind prevailing over the West wind. . . . the socialist forces are overwhelmingly superior to the imperialist forces. . . .' (No Soviet leader has ever made such an unequivocal claim.). Probably Mao's own considerable difficulties with his own industry, agriculture and restive intellectuals all contributed to the Chinese 'leftward' swing in 1957; in the Moscow conference of that year the co-existence line was implicitly attacked by the Chinese. To Peking, coexistence was defeatist revisionism; to Moscow, the hard line was an adventurist dogmatic interpretation of Marxism–Leninism. And the theoretical difference of interpreting 'our era' has never been bridged since that time, despite the drafting compromise of the 1957 Declaration by the twelve ruling Communist parties.

But the cracks papered over in the 1957 Declaration applied not only to global strategy. Peking was also embarking on a hard line in inter-bloc relations, with its persistent condemnation of Titoist revisionism, and domestically, with the 'Great Leap Forward' which was supposed to prepare China for the 'transition to Communism' by regimented 'people's communes' and backyard steel furnaces. (In orthodox Marxist–Leninism, social relations reflect the gradual development of the productive base. Communism will be impossible until there is an abundance of material goods.) In effect, the Chinese by 1957–8 were already staking out a claim to the leadership of the under-developed world. Events in the next three years thus led inexorably to the 1960 split. Against a mounting crescendo of argument and recrimination, hidden in the prolix jargon of Marxist polemics, Khrushchev failed to back Peking decisively in its offensive over Quemoy in 1958, refused to give the Chinese nuclear know-how and samples of the atomic bomb in 1959 — this was the time of the Camp David meeting between the American and the Soviet leader, when Eisenhower was denounced as a fiend by the Chinese Press — and in August 1960 actually withdrew thousands of irreplaceable Soviet technicians from China, together with their blue prints. Already in the Bucharest Conference of July 1960 the Soviet delegates directly attacked the Chinese as war-mongering heretics, dogmatists and factionalists.

As the ideological arguments which were disputed in the Moscow Conference in November 1960 have been repeated endlessly ever since by the two great totalitarian disputants, their content may be briefly mentioned. The Declaration, of course, was far more of a compromise than that of 1957; it combined both views under a Soviet gloss, and the USSR was not referred to as the 'head' of world Communism — as in 1957. For the first time there was no formal centre of Communism, although the Russians had pressured the world Communist parties to back them in isolating the Chinese in the Conference, tactics to which the Chinese had defiantly replied with the reminder that Lenin had been a factionalist when he split the Russian Social Democratic Party.

Basically, this claim to Leninist purity lay at the heart of the Chinese case repudiating coexistence. Unlike the Soviets who claimed that in the present era the 'world socialist system' was through its economic and military resources capable of influencing the development of world society as a whole, the CCP claimed the era was still one of fundamentalist Leninist struggle, not coexistence. This meant that unlike Khrushchev, who saw that war would vaporise Communists as well as imperialists, Peking thought that Communism could emerge from the ashes of war. Most important of all was the differing emphasis on the struggle in the under-developed countries. The Chinese held that the way to power was always through revolutionary 'wars of national liberation' such as those waged in Laos, Algeria, and Vietnam. Moscow, fearing escalation into nuclear war, preferred social, political and economic penetration which would affect state institutions and eventually bring a given country into dependency on the 'world socialist system'. Although Khrushchev, in a post-Moscow Conference speech on 6 January 1961, specifically endorsed 'wars of national liberation', with great flexibility, Soviet ideologists in 1960 also conceived as a stage on the road to socialism the status of 'national democracy', based on the preferred model of Cuba following Fidel Castro's assumption of power in January 1959. Taken together, these doctrinal differences both showed that by November 1960 the split was real and provided the material for intensified conflict between Moscow and Peking.

A full year after the 1960 Conference, when Khrushchev openly abused the Albanian leader, Hoxha, at the CPSU Twenty-second Congress, an event followed by the abrupt departure of Chou En-lai for Peking, the whole world saw the extent of the split. After that, Peking denounced Moscow for capitulationism over the Cuban crisis of 1962, both sides failed to reconcile their major differences in 1963, and by 1964, immediately before his deposition, Khrushchev was thinking of expelling the Chinese from the international movement. By the early 1960s a second, eastern centre of Communism, proselytising the emergent countries, had developed in Peking; yet it would be foolish to forget that the Sino-Soviet split is about rival strategies to destroy the West. And while the great schism developed and proliferated throughout all the world Communist Parties in 1961–2, there would be few in the West who could not see that it was not the guerrilla-minded dogmatists of Peking which were the chief threat, but Khrushchev's missile strategy, taking the world nearer the brink than ever before over Berlin and Cuba.

BERLIN AND CUBA: TOWARDS THE MISSILE CRISIS

Following the abortive Paris Summit of May, and before the showdown with the Chinese in November 1960, Khrushchev maintained the pressure. The Western powers were accused of backing Belgian neo-colonialism in the Congo, the Algerian rebels were given *de facto* recognition, and in September Khrushchev exploded at the UN General Assembly in New York, banging his shoe on the desk as he demanded that Secretary-General Hammarskjöld be replaced by a *troika*: 'There are no neutral men.'

During this time the situation also worsened in Laos, where the pro-Western régime in power since 1958 was overthrown in August 1960 by the neutralist paratrooper, Kong Le. By the end of the year fighting was in progress between American-supported rightist forces on one side and neutralist and Communist Pathet Lao forces on the other, aided by the Russians and the North Vietnamese. By May 1961, when the Foreign Ministers' conference on Laos convened at Geneva, it was clear that the only possible solution which could prevent great-power intervention was neutralisation, even though this solution, which was eventually reached in July 1962, was one which favoured the Pathet Lao and their North Vietnamese masters.[1] But in South Vietnam the situation was also deteriorating; in December 1960, after two years of stepped-up guerrilla warfare, beginning at the end of 1958, and directed from Hanoi, a 'National Front for the Liberation of South Vietnam' was established. From that time on the Communist Vietcong guerrillas never looked back in the prosecution of their externally-mounted 'war of national liberation'.

Yet in spite of the deteriorating situation in Indo-China, a situation which both Moscow and Peking could approve of, 1961 was also the year of the Berlin crisis. President Kennedy

[1] See A. J. Dommen, *Conflict in Laos* (1964), for a survey of the extraordinary complex events in Laos between 1954 and 1964.

1a. The Victors. Stalin, Truman and Churchill at Potsdam, July 1945. Admiral Leahy and Mr Attlee can be seen behind the President.

1b. The Contenders. Kennedy and Khrushchev meet on the steps of the Soviet Embassy in Vienna, 4 June 1961.

2a. Treaty-making. At his desk in the White House, Truman signs the proclamation declaring the North Atlantic Treaty in effect. Representatives of the treaty nations and Secretary of State Acheson look on, 24 August 1949.

2b. Acheson and Dulles stand together in a ceremony as the Japanese peace treaty comes into force, 28 April 1952. Dulles had served as the chief US negotiator on the treaty.

3*a*. Limited War. Amphibious assault in Korea. Carrying scaling ladders to mount the harbour wall, men from the 1st Marine Division head for Inchon, 15 September 1950.

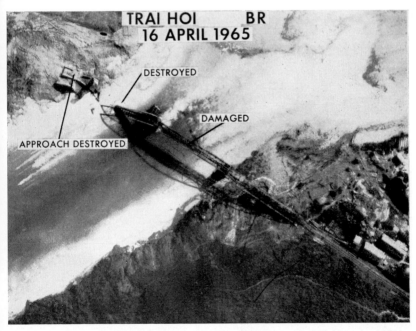

TRAI HOI BR
16 APRIL 1965

DESTROYED

DAMAGED

APPROACH DESTROYED

3*b*. Interdiction in Vietnam. The four-span railroad bridge at Trai Hoi, south of Vinh, North Vietnam, after attack on 16 April 1965.

4. *'Fight Militarism!'* A parade of the 'National People's Army' of the German Democratic Republic in East Berlin. Walter Ulbricht stands on the reviewing platform, 1 May 1957.

Der Kämpfer

ORGAN DER KAMPFGRUPPEN DER ARBEITERKLASSE

5. Jahrgang, Nr. 11   Berlin, November 1961   Preis 10 Pf.

DER KOMMUNISMUS SIEGT!

Die Kraft und Lebenstüchtigkeit des Programms der KPdSU liegt in der selbstlosen Arbeit der Sowjetmenschen / Auch wir haben Anteil an den großen Aufgaben und herrlichen Perspektiven / Die Kämpfer und Kommandeure stehen an der Spitze des Produktionsaufgebotes in der Ausbildung: Mit dem geringsten Aufwand den höchsten Nutzen erreichen

Der XXII. Parteitag der Kommunistischen Partei der Sowjetunion hat einen neuen Abschnitt in der Weltgeschichte eingeleitet. Mit dem grandiosen Programm zum Aufbau des Kommunismus, dem Kommunistischen Manifest des 20. Jahrhunderts, ist der Weg zum Sieg der menschlichsten aller Gesellschaftsordnungen gewiesen.

„Die Partei verkündet feierlich: Die heutige Generation der Sowjetmenschen wird im Kommunismus leben!" So heißt es in der Resolution des Parteitages.

Der gesetzmäßige Übergang vom Kapitalismus zum Sozialismus – das wird im Lichte des XXII. Parteitages deutlicher denn je – ist auch in Westdeutschland nicht aufzuhalten.

Als Hauptergebnis der Tätigkeit der Partei wird im Rechenschaftsbericht die Tatsache bezeichnet, daß es gelang, den Krieg zu verhindern, und daß die Sowjetmenschen und die Völker der anderen Länder die Wohltaten eines friedlichen Lebens nutzen konnten. An anderer Stelle heißt es: Wir glauben, ...

Prozent erzielt haben. Dieses Ergebnis wiegt um so mehr, wenn man berücksichtigt, daß die Kämpfer und Kommandeure dieser Einheit fast ausnahmslos an der Spitze des Produktionsaufgebotes ihrer Kämpfen. Die Brigadeführers von Subo konnte beispielsweise bereits am 21. Oktober die Erfüllung ihres Jahresplanes für 1961 melden. Einen Tag später erfüllte auch die Brigade des Genossen Krumholz den Jahresplan. Beide Brigadiere sind aktive Kämpfer bzw. Zugführer in der Kampf...

6*a*. San Cristóbal, western Cuba, 23 October 1962. A general view of one of the most important Soviet MRBM sites. Since 14 October fuel-tank trailers, missile shelter tents and other equipment has appeared, indicating the speed of the build-up. Note the extensive vehicle trackage.

6*b*. San Cristóbal, 25 October 1962. The build-up continues, as work on the MRBM firing-table progresses.

7a. A U-2 over the Caribbean . . . 'a systematic penetration of the Soviet air'. (See p. 97.)

7b. At a mass rally in Peking 'to support the Vietnamese people's struggle against the armed aggression of US imperialism' Mao Tse-tung greets the head of the mission to Communist China of the National Front for the Liberation of South Vietnam, Nguyen Minh Phuong, February 1965.

TABLE I

ESTIMATES OF COMPARATIVE STRATEGIC STRENGTH EARLY 1965

Figures in brackets are the ISS estimates for early 1964

CATEGORY	WESTERN ALLIANCES	COMMUNIST POWERS
Missile and Air power		
ICBMs	925 (475)	200+ (100+)
Fleet Ballistic Missiles	480 (192)	120+ (100)
IRBMs and MRBMs	—	750 (800)
Long Range Heavy Bombers	630 (630)	200 (200)
Medium Bombers	580 (780)	1,400 (1,400)
Seapower[1]		
Carriers (all types)	37 (38)	—
Cruisers	33 (33)	20 (19)
Escorts	593	1302
Submarines—		
(a) Conventional power	181 (199)	443 (446)
(b) Nuclear power	54 (33)	30 (23)
Land power		
Active army strengths	4,766,000 (NATO 3,121,000)	6,060,000 (Warsaw Pact 3,145,000)

[1] Active fleets or ships in commission
[2] Not all of these are fully manned

8. The Strategic Balance, 1965.

took over in the White House in January 1961, but the first few months of office were clouded by the fiasco of the Bay of Pigs invasion of Cuba. Launched by anti-Communist Cubans in April 1961, the invasion was supported by the Central Intelligence Agency (CIA), and was quickly crushed by Fidel Castro's Soviet-armed forces. Throughout the rest of the year the Soviet build-up in Cuba went on, but the attention of the world was on Berlin. During his first official visit to Europe, Kennedy met Khrushchev in Vienna during 3–4 June, a new, dismal effort at 'Summitry'. In Vienna, Khrushchev's *aide-mémoire* repeated the Soviet demands of November 1958 over Germany, threatening to sign a German peace treaty with Ulbricht and suggesting a demilitarised status for West Berlin. The treaty, which he demanded before the end of 1961, would of course involve East German control of access to West Berlin and thus the abandonment of the West Berliners. . . . The crisis which lasted for the rest of the year, with its undertones of war, was not due merely to the fact that Khrushchev had personally handed the Soviet *aide-mémoire* to Kennedy at Vienna, but also to the uncompromising language of the Soviet ultimatum — for ultimatum it was, couched in uncompromising words, again demanding a Berlin solution on Soviet terms within a period of 'not more than six months':

The years' old delay with the peace settlement in Germany has largely determined the dangerous course of developments in Europe in the post-war period. Major decisions of the Allies on eradication of militarism in Germany, which once were considered by the Governments of the United States and the USSR as the guarantee of stable peace, have been implemented only partially, and now are actually not being observed on the greater part of German territory. Of the Governments of the two German states which appeared after the war, it is only the Government of the German Democratic Republic that recognises and adheres to these agreements. The Government of the Federal

D

Republic of Germany publicly proclaims its negative attitude to these agreements, cultivates sabre-rattling militarism, and advocates the revision of the German frontiers. . . .

Proceeding from a realistic evaluation of the situation, the Soviet government stands for an immediate conclusion of a peace treaty with Germany. . . . The time has already passed when the situation in Germany could be left unchanged. All the prerequisites for the conclusion of a peace treaty matured a long time ago, and such a treaty must be concluded. The crux of the matter consists of who will conclude it and when, and whether this will involve unnecessary complications. . . . If the United States is not prepared to sign a peace treaty with the two German states, a peaceful settlement could be achieved on the basis of two treaties. . . . These treaties need not be completely identical, but they must contain the same provisions on the most important points of a peaceful settlement. . . . The conclusion of a German peace treaty would also solve the problem of normalising the situation in West Berlin. Deprived of a stable international status, West Berlin is at present a place where the Bonn revenge-seeking circles unceasingly maintain a tense situation, and engineer all kinds of provocations that are very dangerous for peace. . . . At present, the Soviet government does not see a better way to solve the West Berlin problem than by transforming it into a demilitarised free city. . . . The existing occupation régime has already outlived itself, and has lost all connection with the purposes for which it was established. . . . The occupation rights will naturally cease to exist upon the signing of a German peace treaty, whether it is signed with both German states or only with the German Democratic Republic on whose territory West Berlin stands. . . . Of course, it cannot be permitted that West Berlin should continue to be used as a base for inciting hostile activity against the USSR, the German Democratic Republic, or any other state . . . the settlement of the West Berlin problem should naturally take into account the necessity of respecting and strictly observing the soverign rights of the German Democratic Republic. . . .

To avoid delay of a peace settlement it is necessary to fix a time-limit. . . . The Soviet government considers that not more than six months are needed for such negotiations. Such a period is quite sufficient for the German Democratic

Republic and the Federal Republic of Germany to establish contacts and to negotiate ... since an understanding of the necessity of putting an end to the vestiges of the Second World War in Europe has matured during the sixteen post-war years. ... The signing of a German peace treaty by all the participants of the anti-Hitlerite coalition and the settlement of the question of a neutral status for West Berlin on this basis would create better conditions for trust between States and for the solution of such international problems as disarmament and others. If the United States does not show that it realised the necessity of concluding a peace treaty, we shall deplore this, and, since it is impossible to delay the conclusion of a peace treaty, we shall be obliged to sign one not with all States but only with those that wish to sign it. The peace treaty will formally define the status of West Berlin as a free city and the Soviet Union, like the other parties to the treaty, will, of course, strictly observe it; measures will also be taken to ensure that it is observed by other countries. At the same time, this will mean putting an end to the occupation régime with all its implications. Notably all questions of communications by land, water, or air through the German Democratic Republic will be settled only by appropriate agreements with the German Democratic Republic. That is but natural since control over such communications is an inalienable right of every sovereign state. The conclusion of a German peace treaty will be an important step towards the final post-war settlement in Europe which the Soviet Union is persistently striving for. ...

In the next few weeks following his return to Moscow, Khrushchev repeatedly attacked the *status quo* in Berlin, while Kennedy for his part returned from Vienna convinced that war might come at any time, because Khrushchev apparently could not be persuaded that the West would fight to support its rights in West Berlin.

Tension continued to rise until on 25 July Kennedy announced a substantial strengthening of the US armed forces, a logical extension of the new conventional warfare strategy of 'Flexible Response' which Defence Secretary McNamara was initiating in the Pentagon. Kennedy unequivocally stated that Berlin 'was the great testing place of Western courage' and that the US would defend its rights 'at all costs'. Moreover, Kennedy made it clear beyond any possible doubt that the US would go to war rather than agree to that 'final post-war settlement in Europe which the Soviet Union is persistently striving for':

Seven weeks ago tonight I returned from Europe to report on my meeting with Premier Khrushchev and the others. His grim warnings about the future of the world, his *aide-mémoire* on Berlin, his subsequent speeches and threats which he and his agents have launched, and the increase in the Soviet military budget that he has announced have all prompted a series of decisions by the administration and a series of consultations with the members of NATO organisation. In Berlin, as you recall, he intends to bring to an end, through a stroke of the pen, first, our legal rights to be in West Berlin and secondly, our ability to make good on our commitment to the 2 million free people of that city. That we cannot permit. . . . West Berlin, lying exposed 110 miles inside East Germany, surrounded by Soviet troops and close to Soviet supply lines, has many roles. It is more than a show-case of liberty, a symbol, an island of freedom in a Communist sea. It is even more than a link with the free world, a beacon of hope behind the Iron Curtain, an escape hatch for refugees. West Berlin is all of that. But above all, it has now become, as never before, the great testing place of Western courage, and will, a focal point where our solemn commitments, stretching back over the years since 1945, and Soviet ambitions now meet in a basic confrontation. . . . I hear it said that West Berlin is militarily untenable. And so was Bastogne. And so, in fact was Stalingrad. Any dangerous spot is tenable if men — brave men — will make it so. We do not want to fight, but we have fought before. And others in earlier times have made the same dangerous mistake of assuming that the West was too selfish and too soft and too divided to resist invasions of freedom in other lands. . . . We cannot and will not permit the Communists to drive us out of Berlin. . . . Soviet strategy has long been aimed not merely at Berlin but at dividing and neutralising all of Europe, forcing back to our own shores. We must meet our oft-stated pledge to the free peoples of West

Berlin. . . . [Kennedy went on to outline the US measures of meeting the crisis, such as supplementary defence build-ups, in conventional forces, and the placing of more strategic bombers on 15-minute alert]. . . . But even more importantly, we need the capability of placing in any critical area at the appropriate time a force which, combined with those of our Allies is large enough to make clear our determination and our ability to defend at all costs and meet at all levels of aggressor pressure with whatever levels of force are required. . . . Thus in the days and months ahead, I shall not hesitate to ask the Congress for additional measures or exercise any of the Executive powers that I possess to meet this threat to peace. Everything essential must be done; and if that should require more men, or more taxes, or more controls, or other new powers. . . . But I must emphasise again that the choice is not between resistance and retreat, between atomic holocaust and surrender. . . . For it is not the freedom of West Berlin that is 'abnormal' in Germany but the situation in that entire divided country. . . . The world is not deceived by the Communist attempt to label Berlin as a hotbed of war. There is peace in Berlin today. The source of world tension is Moscow, not Berlin. And if war begins, it will have begun in Moscow and not Berlin. For the choice of peace or war is largely theirs, not ours. It is the Soviets who have stirred up this crisis. It is they who are trying to change. It is they who have opposed free elections. It is they who have rejected an all-German peace treaty and the rulings of international law. . . . In short, while we are ready to defend our interests, we shall also be ready to search for peace. . . . The Atlantic Community, as we know it, has been built in response to challenge: the challenge of European chaos in 1947, of the Berlin Blockade in 1948, the challenge of Communist aggression in Korea in 1950. . . . If we do not meet our commitments to Berlin, where will we later stand? If we are not true to our word there, all that we have achieved in collective security, which relies on these words will mean nothing. And if there is one path above all others to war, it is the path of weakness and disunity. . . . We shall seek peace, but we shall not surrender. That is the central meaning of this crisis — and the meaning of your Government's policy. . . .

It appears that Kennedy's brave words, one of the two or three most important speeches of his career, at last convinced Khrushchev that the Americans meant what they said; in any case, the crisis could not be maintained at this intensity for much longer, for by July over 10,000 refugees a week were fleeing from East Germany into West Berlin. This threat to the existence of the GDR could only be solved by physical means, and on 13 August the Pankow régime walled off East Berlin from the rest of the city; Allied access rights from the West were not affected. According to Walter Ulbricht, the wall was necessary to keep out of the GDR 'counter-revolutionary filth, spies and diversionists, speculators and traffickers in human beings, prostitutes and corrupted teddy boys. . . .' (*Pravda*, 28 August 1961). Moreover, a new series of Soviet multi-megaton tests, which began in early September, dramatically increased the level of tension and fear all over the world.

But Khrushchev's most immediate problem over Berlin and Germany, that of the stability and very existence of the Ulbricht régime, had been solved by the erection of the wall. For now that the inhabitants of East Germany were literally walled-off from any contact with the West, Khrushchev knew that the crisis need not be carried to the brink. The US announcement, a few weeks after the erection of the wall, that negotiations with the USSR over Berlin would take place after the UN General Assembly convened in mid-September, gave Khrushchev the excuse he needed for withdrawal. Although these desultory talks indicated no weakening of the Western position over Berlin, Khrushchev announced to the CPSU Twenty-second Congress on 17 October that 'the Western powers were showing some understanding of the situation' and thus 'we shall not insist absolutely on signing a peace treaty [with the GDR] before 31 December 1961'. Then, on 27–28 October, in a final, symbolic, Berlin confrontation, American and Soviet tanks faced each other at 'Checkpoint Charlie' on the Friedrichstrasse, before the Soviet armour trundled away; the 'Wall' remained as a brutal reminder of the Soviet hold on Eastern Europe as well as East Berlin, but the Berlin crisis of 1961 was virtually over. Western strength and moderation had triumphed over Khrushchev's bluster.

At the time, with the slowly developing Sino-Soviet schism, it seemed as if Khrushchev's offensive against the West had been called off, a supposition which the protracted Geneva negotiations leading to the formal neutralisation of Laos in July 1962 seemed to encourage. But the greatest crisis of all was in the making in the Caribbean. In July 1962 Raul Castro, brother of the Cuban dictator and Havana's Minister of Defence, visited Moscow. He was followed a month later by the third member of the Cuban ruling triumvirate, the Finance Minister, Ernesto 'Che' Guevara. A USSR–Cuban security treaty was announced by Tass on 2 September; in retrospect the CIA (Central Intelligence Agency) came to the conclusion that the material for the missile sites was already arriving in Cuba, but not until 14 October did a U-2 reconnaissance plane bring back from the San Cristobal area of western Cuba photographs which confirmed to the Pentagon that medium- and intermediate-range ballistic-missile sites were being built there in a crash construction programme.

This is no place to discuss the exact process of Castro's take-over, the best analysis of which is found in Theodore Draper's *Castro's Revolution, Myths and Realities* (1962). Essentially, Castro came to power on the crest of a middle-class revolution against Batista's dictatorship. Once in power in January 1959, Castro soon turned to the extreme left; he needed the Communist apparatus to consolidate his rule, and as an anti-American he needed aid from the Eastern bloc. The Communists, for their part, needed a demagogic *caudillo* — the *Lider Maximo* — to impose their Marxist-Leninist programme on the Cuban people. As Draper rightly sees, it is sheer fantasy to assume that US

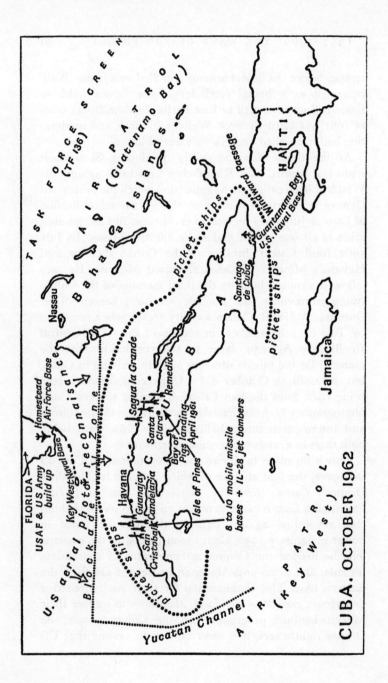

CUBA, OCTOBER 1962

policy forced Cuba into the arms of the Eastern bloc; the crucial decision was probably made in Havana as early as mid-1959, and by the beginning of 1961, when Eisenhower, in one of his last official acts, broke off relations with Havana, Castro's Cuba was, in effect, a Soviet satellite.

Yet Kennedy's reaction to the news of the missiles which pointed at New York and Washington was not that of a man who cared too much about ideology; this was a direct challenge — the most direct challenge so far in the entire cold war — and in the most brutal terms, to the centre of Western power. Khrushchev in a daring gamble of a knight's move had decided to leapfrog the entire NATO defence system, giving Moscow unparalleled leverage, should the manœuvre succeed, in a further confrontation over Berlin. After days of secret debate in Washington, the Executive Committee of the National Security Council decided to blockade Cuba, and in the most historic address of his presidency on Monday, 22 October, Kennedy declared 'a quarantine on all offensive equipment to Cuba'. Should any missile be fired from Cuba against any nation in the Western hemisphere there would be 'a full retaliatory response upon the Soviet Union'.[1] What was at issue now was not Communism in Cuba, but the Soviet missiles which threatened American cities. As the crisis developed in the next six days, the 'Excom' or War Council, debated the

[1] See Appendix D for the Tass announcement of the Cuban–U.S.S.R. security treaty and the full text of Kennedy's broadcast of 22 October 1962. A penetrating study of the missile crisis by Roberta Wohlstetter shows how intelligence of the mounting military build-up in Cuba during September 1962 was partly discounted in Washington 'by the knowledge both conscious and unconscious that the White House had set down a policy for relaxation of tension with the East'. See 'Cuba and Pearl Harbor: Hindsight and Foresight', *Foreign Affairs*, July 1965. Mrs Wohlstetter sums up: 'The Russian performance in the fall and winter of 1962 made it perfectly clear that we cannot take at face value Russian statements—even those made only to the top American leadership in privacy and without these restraints that might be imposed by having the Chinese or other Communist powers or the non-aligned or our own allies listening.'

further courses of air strikes and even invasion of Cuba if the missiles were not withdrawn, and in the Pentagon war-room armed men stood by to shoot down those who panicked. And if Khrushchev should resist with his Cuban rockets, the sites still under preparation on the 26th,

> The American government did not fail to let the Russians know that 144 Polaris, 103 Atlas, 105 Thor and Jupiter, and 54 Titan missiles were ready to convert the Soviet Union into a radioactive heap of rubbish within thirty minutes. In addition there were 600 IRBM and 250 MRBM [medium-range ballistic missile] missiles, 1,600 long-range bombers of various types and 37 aircraft carriers — together three or four times as much firepower as the Soviet Union [could] put into the air. . . .[1]

At the same time there would have been tens of millions of American casualties, and Western Europe would have been devastated. But after an exchange of notes with Kennedy, begun on 26 October, Khrushchev backed down on the 28th. The missiles would be withdrawn, if the United States would not invade Cuba, an offer which Kennedy graciously accepted. The greatest crisis of the cold war, the climax of seventeen years of rivalry, was over. In this Olympian struggle of wills, it was Moscow which had faltered — fortunately — and the world has never been the same since.

THE SECRET WAR

Khrushchev's great offensive, the second great Soviet offensive in the cold war, had been halted, like the first, by the threat of total war. And to recall Truman's defensive victory a decade before, Dean Acheson was one of Kennedy's

---

[1] Henry Pachter, *Collision Course : The Cuban Missile Crisis and Coexistence* (1963), p. 57. Both Theodore Sorensen and Arthur M. Schlesinger have given detailed accounts of the Cuban missile crisis against the general background of the Kennedy Administration; Sorensen, who attended the daily meetings of Kennedy and his advisers during the crisis, is particularly revealing.

senior advisers during the Cuban crisis, carrying the news of the blockade and of the American preparations to the Western European allies. As we shall see in our concluding section, the Cuban crisis was the beginning of a tacit *détente* between Washington and Moscow — a *détente* based on a realisation in Moscow of superior American power. Yet looking back over the Khrushchev offensive, it is impossible to avoid recognising the immense *instability* in the military balance of power between 1953 and 1962, an instability that carried enormous risks. From facts assembled by a well known Sovietologist and a journalist with some access to American intelligence sources[1] we can now see that throughout these years leading to the Cuban show-down there existed a secret technological race between the two competing defence establishments almost analogous to the hidden scientific rivalry between the RAF and the Luftwaffe in the 1930s, which ended in another, earlier historic confrontation in the summer skies of southern England in 1940. Without a brief survey of this race, we fail to appreciate the significance of the Cuban missile crisis.

The story begins a few months after Stalin's death when the Russians achieved their thermonuclear solution at their testing ground Semipalatinsk, in the centre of the USSR. Analysis of the nuclear debris showed that they were driving towards the same sort of weapon as the Americans. But this was only the first development in the Soviet military breakthrough that underlay the new coexistence policy of Stalin's successors. The second development was the invention of rockets that could carry the new weapon to the North American heartland. Even before Stalin's death,

[1] See V. Zorza, 'How the Army Beat Khrushchev', *Life International*, 16 November 1964, and Murphy, 'The Monumental Bluff of Mr. Khrushchev', ibid., 28 December 1964. See especially Robert Conquest, *Russia after Khrushchev* (1965) for the contradictions of the Khrushchev régime, and Thomas Wolfe's *Soviet Strategy at the Crossroads* (1964), for a summing-up of the great Soviet military debate in the early 1960s by a RAND analyst.

repatriated German scientists had told Western intelligence of Soviet missile tests at Kapustin Yar, across the Volga from Stalingrad (as it was known then). But just how advanced was the Soviet rocket programme? It was essential to find out.

By the spring of 1955 the most advanced long-range radar tracking system then in existence had been built by the Americans in north-east Turkey. It showed, as the leaders gathered at the Geneva Summit, that the Russian missiles rising above the wastes of Kapustin Yar were not only intermediate-range rockets, but potentially of ICBM range. Not until a year before, in May 1954, the US had launched its own crash billion-dollar ICBM programme, the obscurely-titled 'Western Development Division' of the USAF. In 1955 the US programme was far behind that of the Russians; there was a possibility that by 1960 the world military balance of power might have swung against the West.

The Soviet missile programme was only part of this nascent threat. The Soviets were also apparently building up a long-range strategic air force. On May Day 1954 the prototypes of the Bison and Badger bombers appeared over Moscow, bombers corresponding to the American B-52 and B-47, and a year later a whole formation of Bison bombers swung over the Kremlin. It was calculated that by the end of the decade the Soviet might possess 500 of these formidable aircraft, and in 1956 there was a public outcry in the United States over 'the Bomber Gap', deriving from the alleged deficiency in the supply of B-52s. In retrospect, it is now known that the Bomber Gap never became a reality, and that the flaunting of the Bison and the Badger may have been a feint designed to make the United States invest in B-52s rather than ICBMs, so giving a decisive lead in missiles to the Soviets. In any case, the Eisenhower administration decided that it must know more about Soviet preparations; there was a high-flying jet reconnaissance plane, designed as a spy plane, on the drawing boards of the Lockheed company, and the CIA thus undertook to organise a programme for what Murphy calls 'a systematic penetration of the Soviet air'.

In June 1956, just before the Suez crisis, Eisenhower authorised U-2 flights for a period of ten days. Flying at a height of 14 miles, the huge cameras of the U-2 looked down on the Bison-Badger airfields and the Volga missile testing grounds. Although the aircraft was tracked by Soviet radar, fighters could not close. In the next four years, until Captain Powers was shot down over Sverdlovsk in May 1960, about thirty extended flights were made over the USSR, and in 1957 the programme was extended to include Communist China. The first task of the U-2 was in assessing the Soviet bomber force, and although the photographs soon confirmed the vast potential of the Soviet air defence command it soon appeared that the Russians had not built up a large Badger and Bison fleet on the pattern of SAC; the bomber-gap was a mare's nest and the B-52 programme was slowed down.

But what about the Soviet ICBMs? Not until the summer of 1957 — as Khrushchev routed the 'anti-Party' group — did a U-2 from Pakistan discover the Soviet ICBMs at Tyura Tam, on the Trans-Siberian railway near the Aral Sea. The U-2 actually photographed the first Soviet ICBM on its pad and recorded the preparations for the first Sputnik; these liquid-fuelled, first-generation ICBMs had enormous thrust, and moreover, the Russians had been testing their warheads for three years in the Arctic at Novaya Zemlya. Then, in late 1957 the Gaither committee reported to Eisenhower that the USSR possessed the capacity to produce by 1959–60 a strategic missile force large enough to destroy SAC and the far fewer missiles the US would have by that time. This alarming assessment (which was not published) was the basis of the so-called 'missile gap' which helped to put Kennedy into the White House in 1961. The real danger was that in this period, which ended with the Cuban crisis, either side might feel so threatened by its opponent's developing strategic nuclear strength that it might embark on a pre-emptive strike or forestalling attack in a new period of tension. For by 1958 Soviet ICBMs had gone into limited production, and this was the military reality behind Khrushchev's great diplomatic offensive that ended in the aborted Summit of May 1960.

But at the very moment of Khrushchev's apparent technological triumph he was decisively overtaken by the Americans. In addition to its first-generation Titan and Atlas ICBMs which began going into service in 1959, ever since 1955 the United States had also been developing the much more sophisticated solid-fuelled rocket systems, the nuclear-powered Polaris submarine which carried sixteen intermediate-range megaton missiles and the Minuteman, which unlike the first generation liquid-fuelled ICBMs, could be dispersed and hidden in underground silos. The Polaris programme, in particular, was pressed forward on a crash basis, following its original inception by Admiral Rickover. To achieve the necessary priorities a three-star admiral, William Raborn — later a director of the CIA — was made director of the programme, which made extensive use of computers to develop all systems in the project simultaneously. By 1959, an American breakthrough in what was a major scientific-technological-industrial undertaking was about to give the United States the ultimate weapons-system, with second-strike capability to retaliate from the depths of the ocean or from 'hardened' missile sites deep underground in the event of a surprise Soviet first strike. These systems went into production under the Eisenhower administration, and by the end of 1960, following the first firing of a Polaris missile from the submerged submarine on 20 July of that year, there were two Polaris submarines on patrol on the high seas; nine were in service by October 1962 when the Minuteman was also operational.

It seems clear that by 1959–60, by the abortive Paris Summit Meeting at the latest, Khrushchev knew he had been overtaken by the Americans in the missile-race that had been going on for seven years. The U-2s had already confirmed that his obsolescent ICBMs had not been put into mass production; only the potential existed for mass production and thus the missile gap had never developed, thanks to the speed of the American recovery. Yet the uproar over the 'gap' was certainly justified as it helped to create a sense of urgency and heighten appreciation of the very real dangers involved in the initial Soviet lead in rocketry. However, as far as Moscow was concerned, 1960 was a year of setback. Soviet industrial production, hampered by the vast capital investment in the missile programme, became stagnant; the failure of the 1959 crop illustrated the historic contradictions of Soviet agriculture, and the consequent termination of economic aid to China, with the withdrawal of the Russian advisers in August 1960, extended the dispute with Peking from doctrinal to state relations, weakening Khrushchev's grip on the international Communist apparatus. Khrushchev attempted to recoup by cutting conventional defence expenditure, so bringing him into conflict with the Soviet military, a conflict that helped to bring about his deposition in 1964.

More important in the short run, this inability to spend more on defence at the very time when the United States was about to switch to the strategy of 'Flexible Response', compelled Khrushchev to take the risks of the Cuban adventure in an attempt to achieve strategic parity with the Americans. But over both Berlin and Cuba, Khrushchev was checked. The USSR with its huge rockets was still formidable, but very much second to the United States, and Kennedy's resolution meant that it was he, and not Khrushchev, who was negotiating from strength as Moscow's colossal nuclear bluff was at last called in October 1962. In reality, the strategy of 'the wave of the future', with its enormous outpouring of resources which the USSR could not afford, had weakened the entire international structure of Communism to such an extent that only in the mid-1960s was recovery visible. It had been the greatest gamble of the entire cold war.

5 1962–1965
The Great Armed Truce

WORLDS OF DIFFERENCE

OVER three years after the Cuban confrontation the main outlines of the cold war were still those foreshadowed in the dramatic exchanges between Kennedy and Khrushchev at the height of the missile crisis. Although neither leader was any longer in charge of events, the *détente* continued, in spite of the Vietnam war. The first concrete result of the Cuban understanding was the nuclear test-ban treaty of August 1963, signed by the United States, the United Kingdom and the USSR. Significantly, the treaty was not signed by China and France, but a valuable corollary of the agreement was the creation of a direct teleprinter circuit, the 'hot line', between Washington and Moscow for use in any further crisis. Paradoxically, the test-ban agreement is all the more significant because it came about not because of any abstract belief in disarmament between the great powers, but because the Cuban crisis had shown, more than any event in the cold war, how great were the risks of the spiralling arms race. For both sides survival is now the primary aim of foreign policy.

Yet the test-ban agreement in no way meant that Communists had abandoned their expansionist aims, or the West its efforts to contain that expansion. 'The fight for disarmament', Khrushchev once remarked, 'is an active fight against imperialism, for narrowing its war potential.' By the mid-1960s, the USSR was not only stronger militarily than it was at the time of the Cuban crisis, building up solid-fuelled and Polaris-type missiles into a second-

strike capability, but the Soviet military were also evolving
their own version of the strategy of 'Flexible Response' to
deal with conventional or brush-fire wars. For its part, the
United States possessed over a thousand ICBMs in mid-
1965, and insisted in all disarmament talks on the preservation of the existing military balance, i.e. one which still gave
Washington a decisive advantage over Moscow. Yet the
policies of Khrushchev and Kennedy were broadly followed
by their successors, and over the Congo, Vietnam, the
United Nations and disarmament itself, there was a subtle
dialogue between President Johnson and Brezhnev and
Kosygin, a dialogue almost amounting to a secret understanding. It was as if twenty years after Yalta, a Grand
Design, a concert of the super-powers, had at last come
about, but one achieved not through amity, or idealism but
through the calculations of *Realpolitik*, readiness to negotiate
from strength, and, it must be admitted, from fear that the
terrible duel at the brink recorded in these pages might
develop from cold war into hot war. The balance of fear
had become the most powerful balance of all.

But as the policies of General de Gaulle and Mao Tse-
tung show, the world we live in today is no longer politically
speaking a bi-polar world, however much the nuclear
thunderbolts are held by the two super-powers. Ever since
Sputnik in 1957 demonstrated the vulnerability of US cities
we have seen that there has been a persistent demand for
some sort of Allied voice in the control of the West's nuclear
forces; what, then, are the chances of common institutions
and policies emerging in the years to come? In May 1962
President Kennedy stated that Atlantic unity represented
'the true course of history', and a few weeks later the same
man, speaking from the steps of the Independence Hall,
Philadelphia, looked forward to a Declaration of Interdependence between the emerging Union of Western
Europe and the old Union of America. To this vision has
been opposed that of de Gaulle — one which Dean Acheson

once termed 'suicidal' — that of united Europe under French leadership, a Europe that would manœuvre as a third force between East and West.

Thus ever since the Anglo-American Nassau agreement of December 1962, which attempted to solve the problem of sharing control of the West's nuclear forces, there has been a lesion in the Atlantic alliance, over the future of its institutions. The Nassau agreement, with its emphasis on Anglo-American nuclear forces, looked back to an earlier age in the alliance; it was answered by de Gaulle's exclusion of Britain from the European Economic Community the following month. But from the Nassau agreement also stemmed the American proposals for the Multilateral Force (MLF), the mixed-manned, Polaris-firing fleet of surface ships, which could give the European allies at least partial control over a NATO nuclear deterrent and thus help to solve the problem of linking power and responsibility.

The French rejection of the MLF (Multilateral Force), and the hesitant British proposals during 1964–5 for a new Atlantic Nuclear Force (ANF) all show the difficulties of developing this control over nuclear forces; moreover the whole problem is also linked to the other great political problem of the West, that of German reunification. The price demanded by Moscow for the reunification of Germany is the high one of the abandonment of NATO by West Germany; if the Bonn government joined the MLF, therefore German reunification would become even more of a chimera than at present. But in any case we must conclude that for the foreseeable future Germany will remain divided on the present basis, an arrangement that with the passing of every year becomes more and more institutionalised. Yet in the dream of Atlantic interdependence, there lies an aspiration that may yet be realised; Britain may yet join the Common Market, and a re-cast Western alliance may still link Western Europe with the United States. In this perspective, in spite of Gaullist nationalism, the cold war may yet bring about some degree of Atlantic political unity, as in the past it has cemented Atlantic economic and military co-operation. Moreover, an Atlantic community might at last convince the Communists that the destiny of the West is not to be buried by history, as Khrushchev once boasted.

But if the West has its 'alliance problems' as it works towards an ever-closer degree of interdependence, these are nothing compared with the fissures in the Communist bloc that have appeared ever since the Twentieth CPSU Congress February 1956. The most obvious analogy with Gaullist nationalism in the Eastern bloc is, of course, Mao Tse-tung's blueprint for a Communist international which repudiates the world of advance technology for a world of struggle where, as Mao once wrote: 'Man, not weapons, decides the issues of war.' For as we can see from the much-quoted exchange which again told the entire world of the schism between Moscow and Peking in the summer of 1963, Peking has resolutely opposed the coexistence policy as a way to Communist victory. In a lengthy polemic entitled *A Proposal Concerning the Chinese General Line of the International Communist Movement* published on 14 June 1963, Peking stressed that all forms of struggle, including 'armed struggle' must be used to attain power:

. . . Can peaceful transition be made into a new world-wide strategic principle for the international Communist movement? Absolutely not. Marxism–Leninism consistently holds that the fundamental question in all revolutions is that of State power. . . . World peace can only be defended effectively by relying on the development of the forces of the socialist camp, on the revolutionary struggles of the proletariat and working people of all countries, on the liberation struggles of the oppressed. . . . Such is Leninist policy. Any policy to the contrary definitely will not lead to world peace but will only encourage the ambitions of the imperialists. . . . Peaceful coexistence cannot replace the revolutionary struggles of the peoples. The transition from capitalism to socialism in any country can only be brought about through the proletarian revolution and the dictatorship of the proletariat. . . .

In reply, the CPSU 'Open Letter' of 14 July 1963 addressed to 'all Communists of the Soviet Union', while approving specific 'wars of national liberation' against colonialism — Khrushchev, with neat dialectical footwork, had always been consistent on this point — went on to reject the Chinese line of *general* revolutionary struggle as 'grist to the imperialist policy of "Brinkmanship" ':

The struggle for peace and peaceful coexistence, weakens the front of imperialism, isolates its most aggressive circles from the mass of the people and helps the working class in its revolutionary struggle and the peoples in their struggle for national liberation. The struggle for peace and for peaceful coexistence is organically bound up with the revolutionary struggle against imperialism. . . . The primary task of the Communist parties is to rally together all those peace-loving forces in defence of peace and to save mankind from a nuclear catastrophe. The socialist revolution takes place as a result of the internal development of the class struggle in every country, and its forms and ways are determined by the concrete conditions of each given nation. . . .

Thus in spite of Moscow's warning at this time that peace-fighters must 'be ready for the armed suppression of the resistance of the *bourgeoisie*,' the fundamentalism of the CCP — strikingly illustrated by Peking's manifesto in September 1965 calling for the encirclement of the West by 'wars of national liberation' — has significantly impressed a north-south bias between the 'haves' and the 'have-nots' over the formal pattern of the East–West conflict. Communist China's explosion of an atomic bomb at Lop Nor in Sinkiang during October 1964 demonstrated the dangers of Peking's ambitions to the rest of South-East Asia. But the Sino-Soviet conflict and China's intransigence towards the established powers do not only reflect the tension between the privileged and the underprivileged, in a world where the industrialised nations are getting ever richer. Mao's policy also represents a nationalist protest against the dominance of Moscow, and his political thought has in effect 'Sinified' Marxism–Leninism in such a way that other Asian revolutionary nationalists can take his work as a general pattern for revolution. Thus the Communist world no longer has a single centre as in Stalin's day, and not only the Chinese but the Poles, the Rumanians and the Hungarians have developed variant, distinctive forms of Communism, albeit still under Moscow's hegemony. The history of the cold war has shown that even inside the bloc, Communism's greatest enemy is nationalism.

The history of the 'uncommitted' nations of the third world has underlined the importance of nationalism. In many ways the new nations have often infuriated both sides in the cold war. To the West, neutralist leaders have appeared ready to combine denunciations of 'neo-colonialism' with an odd disregard of colonialism as practised in the countries of the Communist bloc — colonialism to many neutralist leaders is something which can only happen in overseas territories. Moreover, while attacking the West, many of the states of the third world are run on authoritarian lines, often by military dictators who have destroyed or perverted democratic constitutions. To many in the West, the concept of personal liberty seems low on the collective priority list of the third world.

Yet the new countries have also demonstrated little regard for Communism. In Indonesia, Guinea, Egypt, and Iraq, to name only four examples, generous Soviet aid has by no means inevitably resulted, as it should according to the theory of 'national democracy', in Communist domination. Moreover, Soviet theory, which tries to apply the lessons of Marxism–Leninism mechanically to the neutral nations in general, and to African states in particular, usually takes no notice of local conditions, and, as Leonard Schapiro has written, is 'as little applicable to Africa as to the moon'. And if Chinese militancy has alienated the greatest neutral of all, in the Himalayan offensive of October–November 1962 which destroyed three Indian divisions, Peking's emphasis on guerrilla wars of national liberation has more relevance to the often chaotic conditions of the new countries; besides, the Russians are white men. Given the self-defeating nature of Communist strategy which often appears as the enemy of nationalism, there seems little doubt that if Western policy combines generosity with enlightened self-interest, the uncommitted countries will continue to remain free from Communist take-over. For it is becoming increasingly clear that the great Soviet post-1956 offensive to the third world shows little signs of general success, although no doubt it will continue indefinitely as the only possible strategy available to Moscow.

One way in which the West can attempt to make sure that the third world really remains 'uncommitted' is through the aid programmes of the United Nations, an organisation which, however, has become increasingly inadequate as a means of reconciling political differences between nations. We have seen how the UN Security Council was paralysed by the Soviet veto from the very beginning of the cold war, and how the UN was only able to give its sanction to the American intervention in Korea due to the Russian absence from the organisation in 1950. Realising the Russians would not oblige with the same mistake again, in late 1950 the Allies pushed through the General Assembly the 'Uniting for Peace' resolution which gave the Assembly itself the power to use armed force when the Security Council was veto-bound. Thus throughout the 1950s, under a strong Secretary-General, Dag Hammarskjöld, Western ascendancy in the Assembly was still possible, even if the Security Council was deadlocked. After Suez in 1956, and again in the Congo in 1960, the Assembly set up 'peace-keeping' forces which at least prevented Soviet interference in these areas — although the ultimate sanction against Russian intervention was always American power; when Western policy lacked decisiveness in any area, the United Nations of the Hammarskjöld period was always given the illusion of being more powerful than was actually the case.

With Dag Hammarskjöld's death in September 1961, and with the rising membership of the organisation as the colonial empires were finally liquidated, the West found it impossible any longer to control the Assembly. Many of the new nations, blind to their economic self-interest, were absorbed in their continuing feud with their bogies of neo-colonialism and imperialism. China, from the outside, was contemptuous of the organisation, and Indonesia has left the UN over its dispute with Malaysia. Not only was the Council deadlocked, but the Assembly was impotent. In the summer of 1965, as the largest East–West conflict since Korea raged in Vietnam, the organisation was mute. It had at last become clear to all, that while the valuable relief operations of the UN would continue, the organisation itself could only act in so far as it reflected the wishes of the great powers — a maxim on which it had actually operated ever since 1945. And thus after twenty years it was generally recognised that the UN, like the fragile post-Cuban *détente*, was entirely dependent on the interplay of power, reason — or hostility — between Moscow and Washington.

Yet the war in Vietnam, which intensified during 1965 to the extent that nearly 200,000 US troops had been committed by the year's end, illustrated both the continuity and the essential political nature of the containment policy. As the Hanoi-directed Vietcong insurgents fought to conquer South Vietnam in a 'war of national liberation', and as North Vietnamese regulars increasingly came to be used during 1965, the US military commitment in Vietnam recalled not only the US response over Berlin, Korea and Cuba, but Truman's famous address of 12 March 1947 in which he asserted 'that it must be the policy of the United

States to support free peoples who are resisting attempted subjugation by armed minorities or by outside pressures'. The Saigon régime might not be fully democratic, but to allow the conquest of South Vietnam by the Hanoi rulers through their satellite, the National Liberation Front, would impose an irreversible totalitarian system on the south and would have far-reaching, possibly disastrous results as the credibility of the United States to defend its allies was sapped. In the long run, the fact of Communist-inspired insurgency had to be met in Vietnam, just as conventional aggression had to be repelled in Korea, and nuclear blackmail confronted in the Cuban missile crisis; defeat for the West in any of these cases would have meant a weakening of the world balance of power with a consequent instability in great-power relationships.

In a wider sense, US policy in Vietnam, which had as its objective preservation of the balance of power in the Far East, showed that military action by itself was not enough. In the NATO area, even at the height of the cold war, the West had maintained contact with the USSR through orthodox diplomatic channels and through the UN. With Communist China, there were only the Sino-American ambassadorial talks at Warsaw which were not a real substitute for the many, flexible contacts in the international forums of the world. While not relaxing a military presence in Vietnam, and in South Korea and the Taiwan straits, the United States would not achieve the relative sophistication of its dealings with Moscow until contact with Peking could be widely extended. This would have to wait for the passing of the present generation of Chinese Communist leaders; but eventually the containment policy in the Far East would have to be adapted to include diplomatic as well as military measures if it were to work with the same effectiveness with China as it had with the Soviet Union.

THE COLD WAR PAST, PRESENT AND FUTURE

It would be entirely misleading to conclude this narrative with the assumption that the limited *détente* in East–West relations may become a permanent factor in international life, as some Western analysts believe. There are, in fact, several possible courses the cold war may take in the years to come, and the possibility that there may be a diplomatic reconciliation between East and West is only the first of these alternatives. But, of course, it takes both sides to make a reconciliation; and the briefest study of Communist sources from the *Daily Worker* to the official programme of the CPSU and the 'dogmatist' polemics of the men of Peking will show that to the Communists of both the Russian and Chinese variety an inconclusive ending of the cold war is inconceivable, as the struggle is an expression of the deepest historical reality. In the Marxist–Leninist view, the cold war can only end when one system has at last destroyed the other in a final apocalyptic answer to the question posed by Lenin when he said that all political relations can be reduced to the formula 'Who Whom'? And the Communists have no doubt that the ultimate victory will be theirs, the second possible outcome of the cold war.

Yet again, many in the West believe that if the cold war does not end with a formal diplomatic extension of the post-Cuban *détente* it will somehow come about inevitably through the self-abdication of the Party's ends in a progressive 'mellowing' far beyond Kennan's original hopes of 1947 and that the internal structure of the USSR will, through the influence and demands of modern technology, come to increasingly resemble that of Western countries. This third possibility is even less likely than the possibility that the cold war will eventually end through amicable diplomatic adjustment, and is in fact a Western mirror-version of Marxist historicism, the delusion that history is an inevitable, predictable process that will end in a solution acceptable to ideologues. Those who believe in this internal transformation of the Communist world are the last inheritors of the nineteenth-century view of inevitable progress.

It is true, of course, that there are many grave problems to be solved by the present leaders of the USSR, as Khrushchev's failures with Soviet agriculture, over industrial growth, over the evolution of a suitable military doctrine in the thermonuclear age, and with the demands of the intellectuals for greater freedom of expression, all showed. Communism, in spite of its Utopian origins, is not only an authoritarian creed, dedicated as it is to the unrestrained application and retention of power, but moreover with its obsessional pursuit of unanimity, it is a grossly inefficient doctrine for the operation of complex societies.

Many in the West frequently maintain that mankind's historic drives towards freedom and justice will burst through the tyranny of the Party, yet this view completely discounts the fanaticism with which the Communist leaders hold their creed, and more important, the efficiency of their repressive mechanism and, indeed, the frailty of humanity as a whole. The belief in the gradual erosion of Communist power from within is predicated on a complete misunderstanding of the leverage of the totalitarian apparatus which enables the ruling clique to subjugate an entire society. As a well-known student of modern totalitarianism in both its German and Russian varieties has written:

In 1950 few people had much hope that totalitarianism would disappear in Russia in the foreseeable future. Even now, we know that totalitarian régimes have been defeated in war, and that none has been overthrown from within, and it is difficult to imagine how exactly such a transformation would take place. Those who hope for liberalization as a necessary result of rising living standards are probably mistaken, as were the apostles of enlightenment in the eighteenth century, who expected that the gradual spread of education and knowledge would mean the end of barbarism. There is room for guarded optimism only. A new generation in the Soviet Union may do away with those vested interests which want to perpetuate the totalitarian state. The break-up of the monolithic camp of world Communism may indirectly hasten this process, but nobody knows how this will happen nor, indeed, is it a foregone conclusion that it will.[1]

Much more likely than a true reconciliation between the two sides in the cold war, or a total victory of the values of either of the contestants, is a fourth course, an indefinite continuation of the cold war, with varying intensity of the conflict.

Since the Cuban crisis the Soviet leaders have been playing for time in an attempt to resolve a number of extremely complex issues, both military and civil, which have to be resolved before they embark on a new phase of their power struggle with the United States. Yet this holding operation in no way means that the strategy of coexistence has become one of ideological coexistence with the West. Brezhnev and the centrist leadership which succeeded Khrushchev have reiterated that the strategy of coexistence is the only one doctrinally correct for the world Communist movement, however much they have denounced the fallen leader's '. . . subjectivism and drift . . . harebrained scheming; half-baked conclusions and hasty decisions and actions . . . bragging and bluster; attraction to rule by fiat; unwillingness to take into account what science and prac-tical experience have already worked out . . . (*Pravda*, 17 October 1964).

Thus it may be worth while here briefly recapitulating some of Khrushchev's classic statements on coexistence, statements which are still emphatically echoed by many Soviet sources. Speaking to the Central Committee of the CPSU on 21 June 1963, a few weeks before the signing of

[1] Walter Laqueur, *Russia and Germany* (1965), p. 308.

the test-ban treaty, Khrushchev stated that 'Hatred of class enemies is necessary, because it is not possible to become a good fighter for your people, or for Communism, if one does not know how to hate enemies. . . . Yes, comrades, a harsh class struggle is now in progress throughout the world.' Even at the very ceremony at the signature of the test-ban treaty, Khrushchev reverted to this theme. He spoke of 'the unquestionable fact that opposite social systems exist in the contemporary world. No treaties or agreements between states can overcome the radical contradiction which exists between the two social systems.' Moreover, in one of his last trips abroad as Soviet leader, Khrushchev defined the meaning of coexistence with memorable succinctness: in June 1964, when asked by a journalist during his visit to Denmark when he expected ideological coexistence would be possible, Khrushchev replied: 'Under Communism.'

The lesson seems plain. It is that for the foreseeable future the Communist leaders, for the Sino-Soviet schism is only a dispute over means not aims, will continue to wage their struggle for world mastery. They will persist in their efforts to win over the uncommitted countries, and, much more important will attempt to disrupt the NATO alliance by every variety of divisive political, psychological and military pressures, aimed firstly at the withdrawal of US power from Western Europe and eventually at the isolation and paralysis of that American power which, as we have seen, ever since 1947 has been unremittingly employed to frustrate Communist expansionist ends.

On the other hand, provided the West acts with patience, firmness, restraint and organises its potential in an intelligent manner, then there is no reason why in the long term view, time should not be on its side. Might, we must never forget, is essential for the preservation of right, and in maintaining the balance of power between the two blocs it must be remembered that nuclear capability is not enough.

The American strategy of Flexible Response, the latter-day expression of the containment policy, must continue to be perfected to deal with Communist-inspired limited wars and guerrilla 'wars of national liberation' — all the more likely to occur in periods of nuclear stalemate. Moreover, the West has the greater political capacity to reconcile the nationalism of the third world with its own pluralistic ideals, which in spite of the contradictions in Western society, still offer the world the best hope of freedom, justice, peace and prosperity. Most important of all, thanks to enlightened American leadership, Western foreign policy has succeeded in the last twenty years in containing the Communist bloc by means short of general war. We live not, as Moscow claims, in an age of coexistence, but in an age of containment.

But the possibilities of future Western relations with the Communist world include a fifth and terrible possibility emerging out of what often seems the flux of the last twenty years: nuclear war. The post-Cuban truce, as we have seen, by no means meant the end of the arms race. According to *The Military Balance 1964–5* the forces of the Western alliance then possessed over 900 ICBMs, nearly 500 fleet ballistic missiles, and over 600 long-range heavy bombers, apart from conventional forces totalling well over five million men. In Congressional testimony given in April 1965, Secretary McNamara announced that by June of that year the United States would possess 1,270 ICBMs, including 800 Minutemen in hardened silos, and over 935 intercontinental bombers. In quantitative terms, McNamara went on, the American superiority was 'three or four to one'. At the same time, according to *The Military Balance*, in early 1965 the Eastern powers possessed over 200 ICBMs, 200 long-range heavy bombers, 750 medium-range bombers, and 750 intermediate-range missiles. McNamara's testimony would also seem to imply that the USSR is steadily increasing its ICBM capability.

Moreover, while in the past McNamara has stated that the official objective of the US administration is that the strategic retaliatory forces should be 'large enough to ensure the destruction, singly or in combination, of the Soviet Union, Communist China, and the Communist satellites as national societies, under the worst possible circumstances of war outbreak that can reasonably be postulated', the Soviets have hardly been less explicit. In February 1963, the Soviet Defence Minister Marshal Malinovsky wrote that the USSR would 'answer McNamara's 344 missiles with several times more', and Colonel General Tolubko, Deputy Commander of the Soviet strategic missile forces, asserted shortly afterwards that Russian rockets could 'raze all industrial and administrative targets and political centres of the United States, and will completely destroy the countries on whose territories American military bases are situated'.

Armageddon, then, is certainly a possible outcome of the unprecedented international tensions related in these pages, tensions the inevitable result of Communist political ambitions and conspiratorial techniques engrafted on to inter-state relations which at the best of times would reflect conflicting interests. Marxist–Leninist doctrine, it should be recalled here, continues to recognise the historical dependence of Communism on war, even though Moscow's 'revisionist' interpretation does hold that revolution is no longer 'obligatorily linked' with war. According to the new party programme of the CPSU presented to the Twenty-second Congress in 1961 by Khrushchev, if the global process of evolution to socialism does not effortlessly take place, 'the possibility of non-peaceful transition to socialism should be borne in mind'. Moreover, the internal organisation of the USSR, and especially that of Communist China, helps to generate tensions even in a period of apparent *détente*. Both the Soviet Union and China have created powerful siege economies on a war footing, while the internal mechanism of suppression ensures that the western view of the cold war does not reach the masses, ceaselessly indoctrinated as they are with a theory that assumes that permanent, world-wide strife is the inescapable condition of existence for the foreseeable future. Again, the political organisation of the Communist bloc is such that a small group of men can enforce decisions against the natural tendencies of the population; and this apparatus can be geared to creating conflict as easily as it can be used to promote relaxation of tension.

To sum up; the claim of the Party to speak for history, the internal and external Communist propaganda apparatus ceaselessly disseminating its mendacious view of reality, the totalitarian structure of the USSR and Communist China, the very real threat of the Soviet strategic missile forces, the explosive interaction of the East–West conflict with the anarchy of the 'Third World' and the vast upsurge of inter-racial hatred in the last ten years, all have combined to produce a series of crises that may one day escape rational control, whether by mischance, misunderstanding, madness, escalation, or human fallibility in general. Certainly the risks are enormous until the Communist states decide to live in peace with the West, so making some sort of disarmament agreement possible. Certainly we cannot do better than to base our actions on the words of President Kennedy in his inaugural address on 20 January 1961:

Let every nation know, whether it wishes us well or ill, that we shall pay any price, bear any burden, meet any hardship, support any friend or oppose any foe, to assure the survival, and success of liberty.

Appendixes

A. NATO CIVIL AND MILITARY ORGANISATION

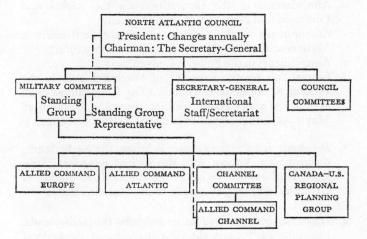

------ Liaison for certain operational matters

B. ANALYSIS OF THE TERMS OF THE LONDON AND PARIS AGREEMENTS, SEPTEMBER–OCTOBER 1954

The Paris Agreements comprise:
1. *Documents signed by two Parties* (France and the Federal Republic of Germany). Subject: Franco-German disputes (the resolution of cultural, economic and other difficulties) and the Saar.

E

2. *Documents signed by four Parties:* France, the United States, the United Kingdom, and the Federal Republic of Germany relating to German sovereignty:

a. Protocol on the termination of the Occupation régime in the Federal Republic;

b. Amendments to the Convention on Relations between the Occupying Powers and the Federal Republic (Revocation of the Occupation Statute, Retention of Rights, stationing of Allied forces, state of emergency, hypothesis of reunification);

c. Amendments to the Convention on the Rights and Obligations of Foreign Forces in Germany;

d. Amendments to the Convention on the Settlement of Matters arising out of the War and the Occupation;

e. Amendments to the Finance Convention;

f. Convention on the Presence of Foreign Forces in the Federal Republic of Germany. (The Conventions cited at a, b, c, d and e above are those signed in Bonn on 26 May 1952, and designed to end the Occupation régime.)

3. *Documents signed by five Parties:* Belgium, the Netherlands, Luxembourg, France, and the United Kingdom. Subject: Declaration inviting the Federal Republic of Germany, and Italy to accede to the Brussels Treaty.

4. *Documents signed by seven Parties:* Belgium, the Netherlands, Luxembourg, France, the United Kingdom, the Federal Republic of Germany, and Italy.
Subject:

a. Protocol revising and completing the Brussels Treaty;

b. Protocol on the forces of Western European Union;

c. Protocol on the control of armaments;

d. Protocol on the Agency of Western European Union for the Control of Armaments;

e. Exchange of letters relating to the jurisdiction of the International Court of Justice;

f. Resolution on the Production and Standardization of Armaments.

5. *Documents signed by the fourteen North Atlantic Treaty countries:*

a. Protocol to the North Atlantic Treaty on the Accession of the Federal Republic of Germany;

b. Resolution by the North Atlantic Council to implement Section IV of the Final Act of the London Conference (authority of SACEUR);

c. Resolution of Association taking note of the obligations accepted by the Federal Republic on the signature of the London Agreements and of the declaration relating to such obligations.

C. CUBAN–SOVIET SECURITY AGREEMENT, 1962

Extract from the Tass Communiqué, 2 September, 1962

During the stay in the U.S.S.R. of Ernesto Guevara Serna and Emilio Aragones Navarro, views were also exchanged in connection with the threats of aggressive imperialist quarters with regard to Cuba. In view of these threats, the Government of the Cuban Republic addressed the Soviet Government with a request for help by delivering armaments and sending technical specialists for training Cuban servicemen.

The Soviet Government attentively considered this request of the Government of Cuba and agreement was reached on this question. As long as the above-mentioned quarters continue to threaten Cuba, the Cuban Republic has every justification for taking necessary measures to insure its security and safeguard its sovereignty and independence, while all Cuba's true friends have every right to respond to this legitimate request.

ADDRESS BY PRESIDENT KENNEDY
Delivered from the White House by television and radio, 22 October, 1962

Good evening, my fellow citizens. This Government, as promised, has maintained the closest surveillance of the

Soviet military build-up on the island of Cuba. Within the past week unmistakable evidence has established the fact that a series of offensive missile sites is now in preparation on that imprisoned island. The purpose of these bases can be none other than to provide a nuclear strike capability against the Western Hemisphere.

Upon receiving the first preliminary hard information of this nature last Tuesday morning (October 16) at 9:00 a.m., I directed that our surveillance be stepped up. And having now confirmed and completed our evaluation of the evidence and our decision on a course of action, this Government feels obliged to report this new crisis to you in fullest detail.

The characteristics of these new missile sites indicate two distinct types of installations. Several of them include medium-range ballistic missiles capable of carrying a nuclear warhead for a distance of more than 1,000 nautical miles. Each of these missiles, in short, is capable of striking Washington, D.C., the Panama Canal, Cape Canaveral, Mexico City, or any other city in the southeastern part of the United States, in Central America, or in the Caribbean area.

Additional sites not yet completed appear to be designed for intermediate-range ballistic missiles capable of traveling more than twice as far — and thus capable of striking most of the major cities in the Western Hemisphere, ranging as far north as Hudson Bay, Canada, and as far south as Lima, Peru. In addition, jet bombers, capable of carrying nuclear weapons, are now being uncrated and assembled in Cuba, while the necessary air bases are being prepared.

This urgent transformation of Cuba into an important strategic base — by the presence of these large, long-range, and clearly offensive weapons of sudden mass destruction — constitutes an explicit threat to the peace and security of all the Americas, in flagrant and deliberate defiance of the Rio Pact of 1947, the traditions of this nation and hemisphere, the Joint Resolution of the 87th Congress, the Charter of the United Nations, and my own public warnings to the Soviets on September 4 and 13.

This action also contradicts the repeated assurances of Soviet spokesmen, both publicly and privately delivered, that the arms build-up in Cuba would retain its original defensive character and that the Soviet Union had no need or desire to station strategic missiles on the territory of any other nation.

The size of this undertaking makes clear that it has been planned for some months. Yet only last month, after I had made clear the distinction between any introduction of ground-to-ground missiles and the existence of defensive antiaircraft missiles, the Soviet Government publicly stated on September 11 that, and I quote, 'The armaments and military equipment sent to Cuba are designed exclusively for defensive purposes', and, I quote the Soviet Government, 'There is no need for the Soviet Government to shift its weapons for a retaliatory blow to any other country, for instance Cuba', and that, and I quote the Soviet Government, 'The Soviet Union has so powerful rockets to carry these nuclear warheads that there is no need to search for sites for them beyond the boundaries of the Soviet Union.' That statement was false.

Only last Thursday, as evidence of this rapid offensive build-up was already in my hand, Soviet Foreign Minister Gromyko told me in my office that he was instructed to make it clear once again, as he said his Government had already done, that Soviet assistance to Cuba, and I quote 'pursued solely the purpose of contributing to the defense capabilities of Cuba', that, and I quote him, 'training by Soviet specialists of Cuban nationals in handling defensive armaments was by no means offensive', and that 'if it were otherwise', Mr. Gromyko went on, 'the Soviet Government would never become involved in rendering such assistance'. That statement was false.

Neither the United States of America nor the world community of nations can tolerate deliberate deception and offensive threats on the part of any nation, large or small. We no longer live in a world where only the actual firing of weapons represents a sufficient challenge to a nation's security to constitute maximum peril. Nuclear weapons are so destructive and ballistic missiles are so swift that any substantially increased possibility of their use or any sudden change in their use or any sudden change in their deployment may well be regarded as a definite threat to peace.

For many years both the Soviet Union and the United States, recognizing this fact, have deployed strategic nuclear weapons with great care, never upsetting the precarious *status quo* which insured that these weapons would not be used in the absence of some vital challenge. Our own strategic missiles have never been transferred to the territory of any other nation under a cloak of secrecy and deception; and our history, unlike that of the Soviets since the end of World War II, demonstrates that we have no desire to dominate or conquer any other nation or impose our system upon its people. Nevertheless, American citizens have become adjusted to living daily on the bull's eye of Soviet missiles located inside the U.S.S.R. or in submarines.

In that sense, missiles in Cuba add to an already clear and present danger — although it should be noted the nations of Latin America have never previously been subjected to a potential nuclear threat.

But this secret, swift, and extraordinary build-up of Communist missiles — in an area well known to have a special and historical relationship to the United States and the nations of the Western Hemisphere, in violation of Soviet assurances, and in defiance of American and hemispheric policy — this sudden, clandestine decision to station strategic weapons for the first time outside of Soviet soil — is a deliberately provocative and unjustified change in the *status quo* which cannot be accepted by this country if our courage and our commitments are ever to be trusted again by either friend or foe.

The 1930's taught us a clear lesson: Aggressive conduct, if allowed to grow unchecked and unchallenged, ultimately leads to war. This nation is opposed to war. We are also true to our word. Our unswerving objective, therefore, must be to prevent the use of these missiles against this or any other country and to secure their withdrawal or elimination from the Western Hemisphere.

Our policy has been one of patience and restraint, as befits a peaceful and powerful nation, which leads a world-wide alliance. We have been determined not to be diverted from our central concerns by mere irritants and fanatics. But now further action is required — and it is under way; and these actions may only be the beginning. We will not prematurely or unnecessarily risk the costs of world-wide nuclear war in which even the fruits of victory would be ashes in our mouth — but neither will we shrink from that risk if at any time it must be faced.

Acting, therefore, in the defense of our own security and of the entire Western Hemisphere, and under the authority entrusted to me by the Constitution as endorsed by the resolution of the Congress, I have directed that the following *initial* steps be taken immediately:

First: To halt this offensive build-up, a strict quarantine on all offensive military equipment under shipment to Cuba is being initiated. All ships of any kind bound for Cuba from whatever nation or port will, if found to contain cargoes of offensive weapons, be turned back. This quarantine will be extended, if needed, to other types of cargo and carriers. We are not at this time, however, denying the necessities of life as the Soviets attempted to do in their Berlin blockade of 1948.

Second: I have directed the continued and increased close surveillance of Cuba and its military build-up. The Foreign Ministers of the OAS in their communiqué of October 3 rejected secrecy on such matters in this hemisphere. Should these offensive military preparations continue, thus increasing the threat to the hemisphere, further action will be justified. I have directed the Armed Forces to prepare for any eventualities; and I trust that, in the interests of both the Cuban people and the Soviet technicians at the sites, the hazards to all concerned of continuing this threat will be recognized.

Third: It shall be the policy of this nation to regard any nuclear missile launched from Cuba against any nation in the Western Hemisphere as an attack by the Soviet Union on the United States, requiring a full retaliatory response upon the Soviet Union.

Fourth: As a necessary military precaution I have reinforced our base at Guantanamo, evacuated today the dependents of our personnel there, and ordered additional military units to be on a standby alert basis.

Fifth: We are calling tonight for an immediate meeting of the Organ of Consultation, under the Organization of American States, to consider this threat to hemispheric security and to invoke articles 6 and 8 of the Rio Treaty in support of all necessary action. The United Nations Charter allows for regional security arrangements — and the nations of this hemisphere decided long ago against the military presence of outside powers. Our other allies around the world have also been alerted.

Sixth: Under the Charter of the United Nations, we are asking tonight that an emergency meeting of the Security Council be convoked without delay to take action against this latest Soviet threat to world peace. Our resolution will call for the prompt dismantling and withdrawal of all offensive weapons in Cuba, under the supervision of U.N. observers, before the quarantine can be lifted.

Seventh and finally: I call upon Chairman Khrushchev to halt and eliminate this clandestine, reckless, and provocative threat to world peace and to stable relations between our two nations. I call upon him further to abandon this course of world domination and to join in an historic effort to end the perilous arms race and transform the history of man. He has an opportunity now to move the world back from the abyss of destruction — by returning to his Government's own words that it had no need to station missiles outside its own territory, and withdrawing these weapons from Cuba — by refraining from any action which will widen or deepen the present crisis — and then by participating in a search for peaceful and permanent solutions.

This nation is prepared to present its case against the Soviet threat to peace, and our own proposals for a peaceful world, at any time and in any forum — in the OAS, in the United Nations, or in any other meeting that could be useful — without limiting our freedom of action.

We have in the past made strenuous efforts to limit the spread of nuclear weapons. We have proposed the elimination of all arms and military bases in a fair and effective disarmament treaty. We are prepared to discuss new proposals for the removal of tensions on both sides — including the possibilities of a genuinely independent Cuba, free to determine its own destiny. We have no wish to war with the Soviet Union, for we are a peaceful people who desire to live in peace with all other peoples.

But it is difficult to settle or even discuss these problems in an atmosphere of intimidation. That is why this latest Soviet threat — or any other threat which is made either independently or in response to our actions this week — must and will be met with determination. Any hostile move anywhere in the world against the safety and freedom of peoples to whom we are committed — including in particular the brave people of West Berlin — will be met by whatever action is needed.

Finally, I want to say a few words to the captive people of Cuba, to whom this speech is being directly carried by special radio facilities. I speak to you as a friend, as one who knows of your deep attachment to your fatherland, as one who shares your aspirations for liberty and justice for all. And I have watched and the American people have watched with deep sorrow how your nationalist revolution was betrayed and how your fatherland fell under foreign domination. Now your leaders are no longer Cuban leaders inspired by Cuban ideals. They are puppets and agents of an international conspiracy which has turned Cuba against your friends and neighbors in the Americas — and turned it into the first Latin American country to become a target for nuclear war, the first Latin American country to have these weapons on its soil.

These new weapons are not in your interest. They contribute nothing to your peace and well-being. They can only undermine it. But this country has no wish to cause you to suffer or to impose any system upon you. We know that your lives and land are being used as pawns by those who deny you freedom.

Many times in the past the Cuban people have risen to throw out tyrants who destroyed their liberty. And I have no doubt that most Cubans today look forward to the time when they will be truly free — free from foreign domination, free to choose their own leaders, free to select their own system, free to own their own land, free to speak and write and worship without fear or degradation. And then shall Cuba be welcomed back to the society of free nations and to the associations of this hemisphere.

My fellow citizens, let no one doubt that this is a difficult and dangerous effort on which we have set out. No one can foresee precisely what course it will take or what costs or casualties will be incurred. Many months of sacrifice and self-discipline lie ahead — months in which both our patience and our will will be tested, months in which many threats and denunciations will keep us aware of our dangers. But the greatest danger of all would be to do nothing.

The path we have chosen for the present is full of hazards, as all paths are; but it is the one most consistent with our character and courage as a nation and our commitments around the world. The cost of freedom is always high — but Americans have always paid it. And one path we shall never choose, and that is the path of surrender or submission.

Our goal is not the victory of might but the vindication of right — not peace at the expense of freedom, but both peace *and* freedom, here in this hemisphere and, we hope, around the world. God willing, that goal will be achieved.

Chronological Table

1943 30 January — Von Paulus surrenders at Stalingrad.

April — USSR breaks off relations with Polish government-in-exile.

November–
December — Tehran conference between Churchill, Roosevelt, Stalin.

1944 6 June — Anglo-American landing in Normandy.

July — Soviet Union sets up Lublin Committee on Polish territory.

October — Churchill–Stalin meeting in Moscow; Japanese navy routed at Leyte Gulf.

December — Fighting between British forces and Greek Communist guerrillas in Athens.

1945 January — Moscow recognises Lublin Committee as Provisional Government of Poland.

February — Yalta Conference; far-reaching agreement by the three allies on the post-war world.

March — Soviet government demands revision of treaty controlling the Straits. Ankara refuses.

11 April — Roosevelt dies; succeeded by Truman.

8 May — VE Day. Allied victory in Europe.

June — Allied Control Council created in Germany. Moscow suggests joint control of the Straits to Turkey.

15 July–
2 August — Potsdam conference.

6 August — Atomic bomb dropped on Hiroshima, followed by second bomb on Nagasaki (9 August).

	8 August	USSR declares war against Japan. Russian troops begin to occupy Manchuria and Korea north of 38th Parallel.
	15 August	VJ Day. Allied victory in the Pacific.
	November	'Democratic' government proclaimed in Soviet-occupied Azerbaijan.
	December	Council of Foreign Ministers agrees on preparation of peace treaties in Europe and allied control council for Japan.
1946	January	Persia complains to UN Security Council over Soviet failure to evacuate Azerbaijan.
	March	At Fulton, Missouri, Churchill denounces 'police governments' of East Europe in 'iron-curtain' speech, says Communism is 'peril to civilisation'. Communist guerrillas (ELAS) in action against Greek government forces. Beginning of Greek Civil War.
	May	US announces that reparations delivery to Soviet zone of Germany to be halted.
	July	Resumption of heavy fighting between Nationalist troops and Chinese Communist forces.
	September	Truman dismisses Henry Wallace from his Cabinet.
	December	Council of Foreign Ministers reaches agreement on European peace treaties, with exception of Germany and Austria.
1947	January	Economic union of Anglo-American zones of Germany created: Bizonia. US withdraws from Chinese truce talks.

	February	Peace treaties signed with Italy, Rumania, Bulgaria and Hungary.
	12 March	Announcement of Truman doctrine of aid to Greece and Turkey.
	June	General Marshall suggests huge aid programme for Europe. Rejected by Moscow.
	July	Kennan's 'Containment' article in *Foreign Affairs*.
	October	Creation of Cominform.
1948	February	Communist coup in Prague.
	March	Brussels Treaty signed between Britain, France and Benelux.
	March–June	Chinese Communists go over to the offensive.
	May	Jan Masaryk found dead.
	June	Tito expelled from Cominform. Beginning of Berlin blockade.
	October	Kuomintang loses Mukden and with it Manchuria.
	November	Truman elected President.
1949	January	Truman announces 'Point Four' aid programme during inaugural address.
	April	North Atlantic Treaty signed.
	May	Berlin blockade ended. Chinese Communists cross Yangtze. Basic Law, establishing West German Republic approved by Western allies.
	August	Soviet Union explodes atomic bomb.
	October	Chinese People's Republic proclaimed in Peking.
		German Democratic Republic established in Soviet zone of Germany.
1950	January	Truman orders making of the hydrogen bomb.

	May	Schuman Plan for West European iron and steel community announced.
	June	North Korean invasion of South Korea.
	September	Western allies agree on measures of West German rearmament.
	October	UN troops, having defeated North Koreans, cross 38th Parallel.
		Chinese Communist forces enter Korea.
	November	CCF defeat UN armies south of Yalu River.
	December	UN troops fall back to 38th Parallel.
		Eisenhower appointed NATO Supreme Commander.
1951	February	UN condemns Communist China as aggressor in Korea.
	April	Truman dismisses MacArthur.
	July	Armistice negotiations begin in Korea.
	September	Japanese peace treaty signed in San Francisco.
1952	February	Lisbon NATO meeting sets ambitious rearmament goals.
	March	USSR proposes neutralised Germany.
	May	Armistice negotiations deadlocked in Korea.
	October	Nineteenth CPSU Congress in Moscow.
	November	Eisenhower defeats Stevenson in US presidential election.
		American thermonuclear device exploded at Eniwetok.
1953	March	Death of Stalin. Succeeded by Malenkov (Premier) and Khrushchev (First Secretary).

June	East German rising suppressed by Soviet troops.
July	Korean armistice signed at Panmunjom.
August	USSR explodes hydrogen bomb.

1954 January — Berlin Foreign Ministers' Conference. No agreement on Germany but Conference to meet again in Geneva to discuss Korea and Vietnam.

April–July — Geneva Conference. No agreement on Korea, but following French defeat at Dien Bien Phu (May), Conference agrees to partition Vietnam at 17th Parallel.

May — Soviet inter-continental jet bomber show in Moscow.

September — SEATO treaty signed at Manilla.

October — Paris agreements end West German occupation régime.

1955 January — Congress 'Formosa Resolution' authorises President to use force to defend Taiwan and 'related positions'.

February — Malenkov succeeded by Bulganin.

May — Western European Union formally established.

West Germany joins NATO.

Warsaw Pact signed.

Austrian State Treaty neutralising the country agreed by the Big Four.

July — Geneva Summit.

September — Nasser announces arms deal with Communist bloc.

December — Khrushchev and Bulganin visit India.

1956 February — Khrushchev denounces Stalin in Twentieth CPSU Congress. Promulgates coexistence policy.

	April	Cominform dissolved.
	June	Poznan riots in Poland.
	July	Nasser nationalises Suez Canal.
	October	Gomulka re-elected secretary of the Polish Party.
		Uprising in Hungary.
	October–November	United Kingdom, France, and Israel attack Egypt, agree to halt invasion after pressure by US and UN.
	4 November	Soviet military intervention overthrows Nagy government in Budapest.
	December	Anglo-French forces complete withdrawal from Suez.
1957	January	Eden succeeded by Macmillan as British premier.
	March	Eisenhower–Macmillan meeting at Bermuda restores Anglo-American relations.
		Treaty of Rome established European Economic Community.
	June	Khrushchev routs 'anti-Party group', emerges as undisputed Soviet leader.
	August	First successful Soviet ICBM test shot.
	October	Soviet space-satellite, Sputnik, launched.
	November	Moscow conference of world Communist parties.
	December	NATO agrees to US proposals for giving missiles to member states.
		First successful American ICBM test-shot.
1958	January–July	Soviet diplomatic offensive. Summit conference proposed.

	July	Revolution in Iraq. US troops land in Lebanon, British troops sent to Jordan.
	July– October	Second Quemoy crisis. Chinese threaten offshore islands. Dulles states US might intervene. Chinese stand down.
	October	Geneva nuclear test-ban talks begin.
	November	USSR demands German peace treaty and demilitarised West Berlin.
	December	Communist insurgents, directed from Hanoi, increase pressure in South Vietnam.
1959	January	Fidel Castro takes over the Cuban Government.
	February– March	Macmillan in Moscow.
	May	John Foster Dulles dies.
	June–July	Nixon in USSR, argues with Khrushchev on merits of democracy.
	September	Khrushchev visits US. Meets Eisenhower at Camp David.
	December	West agrees to 1960 Summit.
1960	January	Khrushchev announces cuts in Soviet conventional forces.
	May	U-2 shot down over Sverdlovsk. Paris Summit breaks down.
	July	US Polaris solid-fuelled missile successfully fired from submarine.
	August	Moscow withdraws technicians from China.
	September	USSR demands *troika* system in UN. Khrushchev bangs desk with shoe in UN.
		North Vietnamese Communist Party demands 'liberation' of South Vietnam.

October	After Cuban provocations, US embargoes trade with Havana régime.
November	Moscow conference of world Communist parties; Sino-Soviet split confirmed.
December	'National Front for the Liberation of South Vietnam' set up by Hanoi régime in South Vietnam.

1961		
	January	US breaks off relations with Cuba.
	April	Abortive CIA-sponsored invasion of Cuba by anti-Communist exiles at the Bay of Pigs.
	May	Geneva conference on Laos opens.
	May–August	East German refugees to West reach 10,000 a week.
	June	Khrushchev meets Kennedy at Vienna. Reiterates Soviet demands of 1958 over Berlin. Gives ultimatum for signing German treaty by end of year.
	June–October	Berlin crisis.
	13 August	East Germans wall off East Berlin.
	September	Soviet nuclear tests in multimegaton range.
	October	Tension over Berlin falls as Khrushchev backs down.
	December	Castro declares: 'I am a Marxist–Leninist until the last day of my life.'

1962		
	January	Organisation of American States expels Cuba.
	July	Geneva neutrality agreement on Laos signed by fourteen nations, including the great powers.
	August–October	Cuban build-up of missiles, technicians and troops from the USSR.

22–28 October	Cuban missile crisis. Following discovery of Soviet missiles on the island, Kennedy forces their withdrawal by blockade and threat of invasion.
October	Chinese offensive, against Indian Himalayan frontier.
November	China orders cease-fire, when Western intervention possible, on 21 November and retreats behind line of control of November 1959.
December	Nassau agreement between US and UK.
1963 January	de Gaulle ends British attempt to enter EEC.
June	Agreement on 'hot line' between Washington and Moscow.
June–September	Sino-Soviet dispute reaches new peak with mutual accusations of betraying revolution.
August	Nuclear test-ban agreement signed in Moscow between US, UK, USSR.
October	Macmillan succeeded by Douglas-Home as British premier.
November	Ngo Dinh Diem overthrown and murdered in Saigon.
22 November	President Kennedy assassinated in Dallas. Succeeded by Vice-President Johnson.
1964 January–June	Heavy fighting in South Vietnam against Communist Vietcong insurgents.

	April	Khrushchev denounces Peking for 'disruptive policy'.
	August	US air strikes against North Vietnam following Communist attack on US destroyers in Tonkin Gulf. Congress 'Tonkin Gulf Resolution' authorises President 'to take all necessary measures . . . to prevent further aggression' in South-East Asia.
	October	Khrushchev deposed by CPSU Central Committee; succeeded by Brezhnev–Kosygin leadership.
		China explodes atomic bomb in Sinkiang.
		Douglas-Home succeeded by Harold Wilson as British premier.
	November	Lyndon Johnson elected US President by overwhelming majority.
1965	February	Escalation in Vietnam. US retaliatory strikes against North Vietnam.
	March	US Marines land in South Vietnam.
	April	President Johnson offers unconditional peace talks over Vietnam, offer rejected by Peking and Hanoi.
		US intervention in Dominican Republic.
		US again reinforces its command in South Vietnam.
		Second Chinese A-bomb exploded in Sinkiang.
	July	President Johnson declares 'this is really war' in Vietnam, and announces US build-up to over 125,000 men. Increasing US air activity in South and North Vietnam.
	August	Disarmament talks on non-nuclear dissemination resume in Geneva.

September   Vietcong monsoon offensive fizzles out in South Vietnam.

Fighting breaks out between India and Pakistan over Kashmir.

Peking announces strategy of encircling the West through 'revolutionary warfare'.

October–
December   US build-up in South Vietnam continues, bringing total of American troops to nearly 200,000 . . .

Bibliography

This is of course a selective bibliography, but most of the books cited here contain a list of further sources.

I. OFFICIAL AND SEMI-OFFICIAL DOCUMENTS, SOURCES AND REPORTS

Foreign Relations of the United States: The Conferences at Cairo and Tehran, 1943. State Department Publication 13675. (Washington, U.S.G.P.O., 1961). The fullest collection of documents and minutes on the conferences available.

Foreign Relations of the United States: The Conferences at Malta and Yalta, 1945. State Department Publication 6199. (Washington, U.S.G.P.O., 1955.) Same series as above.

Foreign Relations of the United States: The Conference of Berlin (The Potsdam Conference), 1945. 2 vols. State Department Publications, 7015 and 7163. (U.S.G.P.O., 1960.) Same series as above.

North Atlantic Treaty: Hearings before the Senate Committee on Foreign Relations, 81st Congress, 1st Session. (U.S.G.P.O., 1949.) Particularly rewarding reading for illustrating the great shift in US public opinion towards involvement in Europe during the late 1940s.

Military Situation in the Far East: Hearings before the Senate Armed Services and Foreign Relations Committees, 82nd Congress, 1st Session. ('The MacArthur Hearings'). (U.S.G.P.O., 1951.) Indispensable reading, not only for the basic issues of the Korean War and MacArthur's dismissal, but for the whole political basis of the containment policy.

In the Matter of J. Robert Oppenheimer. Verbatim Transcript of Hearings before the Personnel Security Board of the Atomic Energy Commission. (U.S.G.P.O., 1954.) A full record, including testimony by almost the entire US defence-scientific establishment of the Truman–Eisenhower period, of the decision to make the hydrogen bomb.

Selected Documents on Germany and the Question of Berlin 1944–1961. Foreign Office Comnd. 1552. (London, H.M.S.O., 1961.) This is the fullest collection of documents available on Germany and Berlin. Contains a narrative.

Report of the Special Committee on the Problem of Hungary. (UN document A/3592, 1957.) Contains much detail on the origins, development and suppression of the Hungarian revolution. Particularly good on Soviet military moves.

Cuba: Statement of Events in Cuba under the Castro régime. State Department Publication 7171. (U.S.G.P.O., 1961.) The case against the Havana régime by the State Department. Reportedly written by Arthur Schlessinger, Jr.

Aggression from the North: The Record of North Vietnam's Campaign to Conquer South Vietnam. State Department Publication 7839. (U.S.G.P.O., 1965.) A synthesis of the available intelligence indicating the extent of North Vietnam's control and command of the war against the Saigon régime.

Survey of International Affairs. Successive volumes, 1947–60. (Royal Institute of International Affairs, London.) This area-by-area review of the period, edited by different specialists, is probably the best available. Indispensable as a reference work.

Documents on International Affairs. Successive volumes, 1947–61. (Royal Institute of International Affairs, London.) Companion volume to the above.

Congressional Record, *passim.*

Parliamentary Debates, *passim.*

The Dethronement of Stalin. Full text of Khrushchev Speech at Twentieth CPSU Congress, February 1956 ('The Secret Speech'). *Manchester Guardian* Booklet, 1956. Should be read for its details of the crimes of the Stalin period. Contains annotation.

The Fundamentals of Marxism–Leninism. (Foreign Languages Publishing House, Moscow, 1960.) The basic guide to Communist strategy.

Marshal V. D. SOKOLOVSKI *et al. Soviet Military Strategy*. 1st ed. (New Jersey, Prentice-Hall, 1963.) Introduced by H. S. Dinerstein *et al.*, of the RAND Corporation. An important book which illustrates how the Soviet military are adapting their doctrines to the nuclear age. Should be read in conjunction with studies by Dinerstein, Garthoff, and Wolfe (see below).

STALIN, J. V. *Problems of Leninism*. (Foreign Languages Publishing House, Moscow, 1953.) The basis of Stalinism, much of it still valid in Soviet theory and practice.

2. MEMOIRS, AUTOBIOGRAPHIES, BIOGRAPHIES, SPEECHES

ACHESON, DEAN. *Power and Diplomacy*. (Cambridge, Mass., Harvard U.P., 1958.) Collected lectures.

— *Sketches from Life*. (London, Hamish Hamilton, 1961.) The former Secretary of State's memoirs. Much too short.

ADAMS, SHERMAN. *Firsthand Report*. (New York, Harper, 1961.) Eisenhower's grey eminence in the 1952 Presidential Election and the successive crises until his resignation in 1958. A basic source book.

BERLIN, ISAIAH. *Karl Marx*. (London, O.U.P., 1949.) The classic study of Marx.

BUNDY, W. McGEORGE. *The Pattern of Responsibility*. (Boston, Houghton Mifflin, 1952.) Acheson's major speeches.

BYRNES, JAMES F. *Speaking Frankly*. (New York, Harper, 1947.) Truman's Secretary of State, 1945–47, discusses the beginnings of the cold war. Much interesting material on the deterioration of Soviet-American relations.

CHURCHILL, WINSTON S. *The Second World War*. 6 vols. (London, Cassell, 1948–54.) See especially vol. vi, *Triumph and Tragedy*, for Churchill's unique account of the end of the Grand Alliance. See particularly the account of Yalta and Potsdam.

DJILAS, MILOVAN. *Conversations with Stalin*. (London, Penguin, 1963.) Djilas's disillusion from partisan days to the break with Moscow in 1948. A vivid study of the 'greatest criminal in history'.

DONOVAN, ROBERT J., *Eisenhower: The Inside Story*. (New York, Harper, 1956.) A 'campaign history' for the 1956 presidential election which contains much interesting detail on Eisenhower's first term.

DULLES, JOHN FOSTER. *War or Peace*. (New York, Macmillan, 1950.) Should be read for Dulles's fundamentally idealistic approach to diplomacy. Best read in conjunction with Acheson's *Power and Diplomacy*.

EDEN, SIR ANTHONY. *Full Circle*. (London, Cassell, 1960.) From the Korean truce negotiations to Suez via German rearmament, and the Geneva conferences of 1954 and 1955. Interesting for Eden's account of how the Paris agreements of 1954 were reached.

EISENHOWER, D. D. *The White House Years*, vol. i, *Mandate for Change 1953–1956*. (London, Heinemann, 1963). Vol. ii, *Waging Peace 1956–1961*. (London, Heinemann, 1966.) Disappointing, but better on foreign than domestic problems.

FORRESTAL, JAMES. *The Forrestal Diaries*. Ed. by Walter Millis and E. S. Duffield. (New York, Viking, 1951.) A basic source book for the period put together from the papers of the first Secretary of Defence, who died by his own hand in 1949. Especially good on the formulation of the containment policy.

GOOLD-ADAMS, RICHARD. *The Time of Power: A Reappraisal of John Foster Dulles*. (London, Weidenfeld & Nicolson, 1962.) A detailed, comprehensive and sympathetic study of Dulles and his secretaryship. The best account of Dulles to date.

HUGHES, EMMET J. *The Ordeal of Power*. (London, Macmillan, 1963.) A critical, brilliant, and absorbing account of the Eisenhower years by one of the former president's speech writers.

KHRUSHCHEV, N. S. *For Victory in Peaceful Competition with Capitalism*, a collection of speeches. (New York, E. P. Dutton, 1960.) Title speaks for itself.

MACARTHUR, DOUGLAS. *Reminiscences*. (London, Heinemann, 1964.) Little new on MacArthur's career to 1945, but revealing on the extent of his differences with Truman over the strategy of the Korean War.

Mao Tse-tung. *Selected Works*. 4 vols. (London, Lawrence & Wishart, 1954–6.) Should be read in conjunction with Schram's study (see below).

Murphy, Robert. *Diplomat Among Warriors*. (London, Collins, 1964.) The State Department's senior trouble-shooter tells the inside story of the Berlin Air Lift, the Japanese peace treaty, Suez and Middle East crisis of 1958.

Nixon, Richard. *Six Crises*. (London, Allen, 1962.) Nixon's study conveys much of the atmosphere of the Eisenhower period.

Schlesinger, Arthur M., Jr. *A Thousand Days: John F. Kennedy in the White House*. (London, Deutsch, 1965.) A brilliant portrait in the great tradition of historical writing. Author's *bête noire*: the Department of State.

Schram, Stuart R. *The Political Thought of Mao Tse-tung*. (London, Pall Mall Press, 1963.) The best study to date by a Chinese expert who often compares the official version of Mao's writings with their sometimes different original text.

Sherwood, Robert. *Roosevelt and Hopkins*. (New York, Harper, 1948.) Edited from the Harry Hopkins papers. Sherwood's study is most important for assessing Roosevelt's policy towards the Russians. Excellent account of Yalta.

Sorensen, Theodore. *Kennedy*. (London, Hodder & Stoughton, 1965.) The fullest biographical study to date by one of the late President's closest associates. Especially good on the Cuban missile crisis.

Strauss, Lewis *Men and Decisions*. (London, Macmillan, 1962.) A former chairman of the US Atomic Energy Commission tells of the war-time work on the atomic bomb, the decision to build the H-bomb, and nuclear developments in the 1950s.

Truman, Harry S. *Memoirs*, vol. i, *Year of Decision, 1945*; vol. ii, *Years of Trial and Hope 1946–53*. (London, Hodder & Stoughton, 1955 and 1956.) Splendid, honest, dramatic memoirs by the greatest decision-maker of the cold war.

Vandenberg. *The Private Papers of Senator Vandenberg*. ed. by Arthur Vandenberg, Jr., with V. A. Morris. (London,

Gollancz, 1953.) Much information on the evolution of the Marshall Plan and NATO by a much-respected Republican Chairman of the Senate Foreign Relations Committee. Written from the Senate's viewpoint throughout.

3. SECONDARY SOURCES

BELL, CORAL. *Negotiation from Strength*. (London, Chatto & Windus, 1962.) A study of the whole problem of 'negotiating from strength' since its inception in 1950. Most perceptive on evolution of US and Russian strategy.

BLACK, CYRIL, and THORNTON, THOMAS (eds.), *Communism and Revolution: The Strategic uses of Political Violence*. (New Jersey, Princeton U.P., 1964.) A comprehensive survey of Communist strategy and tactics since 1945. Covers most of the world; exposition of Communist theory is excellent.

BRANDT, CONRAD. *Stalin's Failure in China 1924–7*. (Cambridge, Mass., Harvard, U.P., 1958.) Useful in assessing the later histories of the Kuomintang and the CCP.

BULL, HEDLEY. *The Control of the Arms Race*. (London, Weidenfeld & Nicolson, 1961.) A full survey of the problems involved.

CAREW-HUNT, R.N. *The Theory and Practice of Communism*. Revised ed. (London, Pelican, 1963.) An able survey of the development of Communist theory from Marx to Stalin.

CLEWS, J. C. *Communist Propaganda Techniques*. (Methuen, 1964.) Penetrating survey of this complex subject. Contains list of Communist bloc publications, and front organisations. Certain to remain a standard work.

CONQUEST, ROBERT. *Power and Policy in the U.S.S.R.* (London, Macmillan, 1961.) Following a well-documented analysis of the struggle for power in the USSR, the author describes the Leningrad Case, The Doctor's Plot, Beria's Fall, the Anti-Party group and Khrushchev's rise to power.

——. *Russia After Khrushchev*. (London, Pall Mall Press, 1965.) Brings the story up to date . . .

CROZIER, BRIAN. *The Rebels*. (London, Chatto & Windus,

1960.) A general study of post-insurrections by a former Reuter correspondent in South-East Asia.

DALLIN, DAVID. *Soviet Espionage.* (London, O.U.P., 1955.) Contains a vast amount of material on Moscow's world-wide spy apparatus.

DINERSTEIN, HERBERT S. *War and the Soviet Union.* Revised ed. (New York, Praeger, 1962.) Thorough survey of Soviet views on surprise nuclear attack and nuclear war based on Soviet material by a RAND expert.

DOMMEN, ARTHUR J. *Conflict in Laos: The Politics of Neutralisation.* (London, Pall Mall Press, 1964.) Clarifies the extremely complex events of 1954–64.

DONNELLY, DESMOND. *The Struggle for the World.* (London, Collins, 1965.) A general survey of the cold war 'since its inception in 1917'.

DRAPER, THEODORE. *Castro's Revolution: Myths and Realities.* (New York, Praeger, 1962.) The historian of the American Communist Party analyses Castro's rise to power. Possibly the best book on the subject to date.

ERICKSON, JOHN. *The Soviet High Command.* (London, Macmillan, 1962.) The definitive work; ends in 1941.

FAINSOD, MERLE. *How Russia is Ruled.* Revised ed. (London, O.U.P., 1963.) The most complete account available of the structure of the CPSU and the Soviet state by the professor of government at Harvard.

FALL, BERNARD B. *The Two Vietnams: A Political and Military Analysis.* (London, Pall Mall Press, 1963.) A full account of the two warring Vietnamese states to 1963.

FINER, HERMAN. *Dulles Over Suez.* (London, Heinemann, 1964.) An angry, anti-Dulles study of great length; contains much information and many references to the relevant sources.

FITZGERALD, C. P. *The Birth of Communist China.* (Originally published as *Revolution in China.*) (London, Pelican, 1964.) Interesting in that it points out how historical factors peculiar to China facilitated the transition to Communism.

GARTHOFF, RAYMOND. *Soviet Strategy in the Nuclear Age.* Revised ed. (New York, Praeger, 1962.) A comprehensive study of the intellectual basis of Soviet military strategy. Cf. Dinerstein's study (see above).

GREENE, T. N. *The Guerrilla — and how to fight him.* (*Marine Corps Gazette*, New York, Praeger, 1962.) Contains essays on insurgency and counter-insurgency in Greece, Malaya, Indo-China, Cuba by various experts including Professor W. W. Rostow. Good bibliography. President Kennedy called this collection an 'outstanding presentation'.

GOLDMAN, ERIC. *The Crucial Decade: America 1945–55.* (New York, Knopf, 1956.) Professor Goldman's book is especially good on the 1949–52 period in US domestic politics.

HAMMOND, THOMAS T. (ed.). *A Bibliography on Soviet Foreign Relations and World Communism.* (New Jersey, Princeton U.P., 1964.) Contains 7,000 books in twenty-five languages with specialist annotation.

HONEY, P. J. *Communism in North Vietnam.* (Massachusetts Institute of Technology Press, 1963.) The standard book on the Democratic Republic of Vietnam. Uses for the most part Communist sources.

KAHN, HERMAN. *On Thermonuclear War.* (New Jersey, Princeton U.P., 1960.) The blue-print of Armageddon. Outstanding for its clarity and dispassionate approach.

KAUFMANN, WILLIAM W. *The McNamara Doctrine.* (New York, Harper, 1964.) Written by an aide close to the Secretary of Defence, and thus may be taken as the authorised version of the doctrine.

KISSINGER, HENRY. *Nuclear Weapons and Foreign Policy* (Council on Foreign Relations, New York, Harper, 1957.) The seminal book on strategy and foreign policy. Inspired by Dulles's 'Massive Retaliation' speech, which apparently precluded strategic options.

LAQUEUR, WALTER. *Russia and Germany.* (London, Weidenfeld & Nicolson, 1965.) Excellent historical survey.

LICHTHEIM, GEORGE. *Marxism: A Historical and political study.* (London, Routledge & Kegan Paul, 1961.) A penetrating analysis of Marxism and its application in practice from 1848 to 1948.

LUARD, EVAN (ed.), *The Cold War: A Reappraisal.* (London,

Thames & Hudson, 1964.) Wide-ranging symposium on all fronts of the cold war by well-known experts.

MACKINTOSH, MALCOLM. *Strategy and Tactics of Soviet Foreign Policy*. (London, O.U.P., 1962.) A most thorough and illuminating analysis of Soviet diplomacy, strategy and military doctrine from 1944 to 1961. Pays special attention to the shifts in military strategy.

The Military Balance, 1964–65. (Institute for Strategic Studies, London, 1965.) A standard work, published annually, and one which gives the most general evidence available of the extent of the arms race.

NORTH, ROBERT. *Moscow and the Chinese Communists*. (California, Stanford U.P., 1953.) Essential for understanding Stalin's role in Chinese events.

PACHTER, HENRY. *Collision Course: The Cuban Missile Crisis and Coexistence*. (New York, Praeger, 1963.) A narrative of the crisis followed by an analysis linking the political and military aspects of confrontation as seen from Moscow, Washington, and Havana.

REES, DAVID. *Korea: The Limited War*. (London, Macmillan, 1964.) A general survey of the conflict against the background of the cold war.

ROBERTSON, TERENCE. *Crisis: The Inside Story of the Suez Conspiracy*. (London, Hutchinson, 1965.) Using high French and Israeli sources a Canadian journalist tells the story of the secret alliance against Egypt in 1956.

ROSTOW, W. W. *The United States in the World Arena*. (New York, Harper, 1961.) Professor Rostow was chairman of the State Department's Policy Planning Staff. A particularly good survey.

SCALAPINO, ROBERT (ed.). *North Korea Today*. (New York, Praeger, 1963.) Contains a series of detailed studies on North Korea; best introduction available.

SCHAPIRO, LEONARD. *The Communist Party of the Soviet Union*. (London, Eyre & Spottiswoode, 1960.) Likely to remain for many years as the most reliable history of CPSU, a survey which begins with the nineteenth-century revolutionaries.

SCHWARTZ, BENJAMIN. *Chinese Communism and Rise of Mao*.

Revised ed. (Cambridge, Mass., Harvard U.P., 1958.) Although this book deals in some detail with the crucial years of 1930–5 in the story of the CCP, it also contains in the final chapter a most detailed analysis of 'Maoism' as a new development of Marxism–Leninism.

SETON-WATSON, HUGH. *Neither War Nor Peace.* (London, Methuen, 1960.) A seminal study of the forces in the post-1945 world by a most perceptive historian. See also his *Pattern of Communist Revolution.* (Methuen, 1953.)

SHULMAN, MARSHALL D. *Stalin's Foreign Policy Reappraised.* (Cambridge, Mass., Harvard U.P., 1963.) Particularly good on the development of the Soviet 'peace' offensive after 1949, and the international atmosphere of Stalin's last years.

SMITH, JEAN EDWARD. *The Defence of Berlin.* (O.U.P., New York, 1963.) The best study to date of the Berlin problem. Particularly good on the 1958–61 crisis.

STRANSKY, J. *East Wind over Prague* (London, Hollis & Carter, 1950.) A contemporary account of the Communist take-over in Czechoslovakia.

TANG TSOU. *America's Failure in China, 1941–1950.* (Chicago U.P., 1963.) An intensely dramatic and well documented study by a Chinese scholar living in the US of the fall of the Kuomintang and US dealings with China.

WOLFE, THOMAS W. *Soviet Strategy at the Crossroads.* (Cambridge, Mass., Harvard U.P., 1964.) A detailed analysis of the great Soviet defence debate as seen by a RAND expert. Based mainly on Soviet sources. Cf. Garthoff and Dinerstein (above).

XYDIS, STEPHEN G. *Greece and the Great Powers, 1944–1947. Prelude to the 'Truman Doctrine'.* (Salonika, Institute for Balkan Affairs, 1963.) Impossible to understand the formulation of the Truman Doctrine without reading this book. Brings out how US policy towards intervention in Greece was already changing in 1946.

ZAGORIA, DONALD S. *The Sino-Soviet Conflict 1956–61.* (With a new preface.) First published 1962. (New York, Athenaeum/Princeton U.P., 1964.) The great schism from its beginnings in theory and practice. For further developments see William E. Griffith, *The Sino-Soviet Rift* (London, Allen & Unwin, 1964); and *Sino-Soviet Relations, 1964–65*, same author, *China Quarterly*, No. 25, Jan.–March 1966.

ZAWODNY, J. K. *Deaths in the Forest*. (Indiana, University of Notre Dame Press, 1963.) A definitive survey of the evidence surrounding the Katyn massacre; leaving little doubt as to the responsibility of the NKVD.

4. PRESS, PERIODICAL ARTICLES, AND OFFICIAL JOURNALS

The China Quarterly, London, *passim*.

Congressional Record, *passim*.

Foreign Affairs, New York, *passim*, see especially
July 1947; 'The Sources of Soviet Conduct', by Mr. 'X' (George Kennan). As relevant today as it was in 1947 in understanding Soviet policy.
January 1959; 'The Delicate Balance of Terror', by Albert Wohlstetter. A seminal study of the mechanics of surprise attack which has had much influence on US strategic doctrine.
July 1965; 'Cuba and Pearl Harbor: Hindsight and Foresight', by Roberta Wohlstetter. Using intelligence material revealed in Congressional hearings, this study shows how preconceptions influenced interpretation of Cuban warning signals, so giving the USSR strategic surprise.

House of Commons Debates (Hansard), *passim*.

Life, New York.
'A Policy of Boldness', John Foster Dulles, 19 May 1952. The 'Liberation' policy outlined.
'How Dulles Averted War', James Shepley, 16 January 1956. The 'Brinkmanship' article.
'How the Army Beat Khrushchev', Victor Zorza, 16 November 1964. A summing-up of the Soviet defence debate of the early 1960s. (*Life International*.)
'The Monumental Bluff of Mr. Khrushchev', Charles

J. V. Murphy, 28 December 1964. The U-2 story and the struggle for missile supremacy. (*Life International.*)

Problems of Communism, USIS, Washington, *passim.*

Survey: A Journal of Soviet and East European Studies, London, *passim.*

In addition, the weekly *State Department Bulletin* prints the text of many US official statements, documents and speeches; while the *Current Digest of the Soviet Press* (1949–), published weekly in New York under the joint auspices of the American Council of Learned Societies and the Social Science Research Council, provides translations of selected articles from the Soviet press, as well as a weekly index to *Pravda* and *Izvestiya.* For Communist China there is a wide selection of translations available in *Current Background, Selections from China Mainland Magazines*, and *Survey of the China Mainland Press*, all published in mimeographed form by the US Consulate-General in Hong Kong.

Index